ABOUT THE AUTHOR . . .

The man who presides over the Department of Religious Education at Catholic University in Washington, D. C., and who has been largely instrumental in changing the entire approach of teaching religion in the United States is Father Gerard S. Sloyan. His one goal is to renovate for U.S. Catholics an outdated, inadequate, often defeatist approach to the teaching of religion.

As head of the Department, his biggest task is to bring about this change of pace wisely and within the norms set by Vatican II. Catechetics, Father Sloyan makes clear, is just a big word describing the whole educational program for spreading the gospel—the good news of Christ. "This means," he explains, "that the Christian is on his own. The burden of freely deciding what he shall do and be is primarily the individual's. This is the job of the modern catechetics: to help people come to know who they are and what are the conditions for the best exercise of their freedom."

Using this same free, open, and direct approach, Father Sloyan explains in WORSHIP IN A NEW KEY just what the constitution on the sacred liturgy can mean to each of us.

"Father Sloyan's new book, WORSHIP IN A NEW KEY, is for everybody. Coming from a liturgical scholar quite capable of communication, it brings the renewal and especially the new *Constitution on the Liturgy* to a sharp, practical focus."

Archbishop Paul J. Hallinan

Worship in a New Key

•

WHAT THE COUNCIL TEACHES
ON THE LITURGY

•

GERARD S. SLOYAN

ECHO BOOKS

A DIVISION OF DOUBLEDAY & COMPANY, INC.

GARDEN CITY, NEW YORK

Echo Books edition published October 1966
by special arrangement with Herder and Herder, New
York

Echo Books edition: 1966

Acknowledgment is hereby made to H. M. Mackin, generous publisher of *Hi-Time,* where the first version of
these chapters largely appeared. The concern of this peri-
odical for liturgical renewal has been firm and constant.

For Jean and Virginia

Contents

8   *Contents*

Worship in a New Key

1. What Is the
Constitution on the Sacred Liturgy?

The Constitutional Convention met in Philadelphia from May 25, 1787, to September 17 of the same year, when thirty-nine of the forty-two delegates signed the Constitution and sent it to Congress. It took another nine months for the ninth state to ratify it (New Hampshire, in June, 1788). This made the Constitution the law of the land. Virginia, New York, and North Carolina came into line later that year, and Rhode Island finally approved the document in May, 1790.

This brief recall of United States history should help us understand the historic events that have been taking place in the life of the Church in the last few years. An important difference is that the population of the thirteen original states in 1790 was just short of four million people, whereas the Catholics of the world are just over 572 millions. The Orthodox, Anglican, and Protestant Christians affected by what is happening at Vatican Council II number some 358 millions more.

There is a difference of still greater importance between the early political situation in the United States and the international Christian situation. It is this: not only is the Holy Spirit at work in the Church in a way that He is not among governments of men (although many, indeed most, governments have good will, and He is at work among them), but there is also the question of what effect a change in law or practice will have on the lives of millions of believers who are very sensitive about anything that touches their religious lives. It is one thing to threaten the commercial interests of a new New England state with "federalism." It is quite another to propose to all the people of Italy or Ireland that they celebrate Mass quite differently from the way they have been doing it for over five hundred years—in its basic rite, over fifteen hundred.

Pope John XXIII, in a letter dated December 25, 1961, called a meeting of all the bishops of the world who were united with him in faith and discipline. The announcement made a great many people unhappy. He was an old man, some said; they even hinted that he didn't "have all his buttons." In any case, he was rocking the boat—Peter's boat. Hadn't the Church been getting along all right without a council? After all, there was one just a little while ago (Vatican I, 1869–1870). Besides, the Church settled all the important issues at the Council of Trent, held the day before yesterday (1545–1563), didn't she? Or did she?

Pope John said she didn't. The twentieth century was a new day—*giorno* (johr′-no) was the way he said it. What the Church desperately needed in this century was to be brought up to date—have an *aggiornamento* (aj-johr-na-men′-to).

Well, they got busy in Rome all during the winter and spring of 1962, doing what the Pope had asked. They got reasonably busy, that is. Nothing fanatical, understand. A number of commissions were set up to prepare agenda (that is, things to discuss and vote on) for the fathers of the Council when they assembled the following autumn. There was work to be done by skilled theologians in almost every area you can think of: Christian unity, the Mass and the other sacraments, the nature of the Church, the roles of bishops, priests, and laymen.

There were commissions on movies and television, on the relations between Church and world, on education in seminaries. There were no study groups set up on world peace, however, or population, or poverty. Pope John gave as his reason that he wanted to attend to problems of the Church's interior life and structure first. He clearly hoped that the impact of the Council would be felt on the other Christian bodies, and on world affairs in general, once the members of the Roman Church looked carefully into their own appreciation of the gift of faith and what they were doing about it.

The Council opened on October 11, 1962. Most of the Council fathers are bishops. Some abbots and superiors of religious congregations of men ("fathers general") were also there—at the highest peak of attendance, about 2,365 in all.

There are no women representing the Church in the Council, and no laymen, except as "auditors." The women, some sisters among them, were added during the third session (1964).

At the first session, which closed on December 7, 1962, there were several dozen official observers from the non-Catholic Christian bodies which had accepted Pope John's invitation. Seated with them was one French Catholic layman named Jean Guitton, a writer.

The steering committee of the Council proposed as its first subject for discussion the liturgy of the Church. There were several reasons for this. Many fathers thought that the sacramental prayer-life of Christians was supremely important; therefore, "First things first." Some thought it a nice, quiet topic that couldn't be discussed heatedly, therefore one that would keep theological or other really "important" matters from reaching the Council floor in a hurry. But the chief reason that the liturgy came up first seems to be that the preparatory commission on this subject had done its homework better than any of the others!

Debate on the liturgy continued from October 22 to November 13, 1962, at the first session. The fathers discussed the matter of the language used in liturgy for a long time; also, the place of the Bible in worship, how to adapt Western and Roman prayer forms to other peoples and parts of the world, and how to rearrange the Mass and other celebrations so that all the people would do their parts and not just the priest and sacred ministers and choir do everything for the people. On November 14, a vote of 2,162 to 46 favored the general line taken in the *schema* on liturgy.

The Council went on to discuss God's revelation, communications media, the unity of Christians, and the Church. Then, on the last working day of the session, there was a vote taken on the first chapter (there came to be seven altogether) of the document on the liturgy, "General Norms and Principles." It passed with only eleven negative votes. Another 188 fathers approved the chapter generally but had a few private reservations.

All during the second session in the fall of 1963 the Council fathers voted on the next six chapters of the *Constitution* while they were debating other questions. Finally, on the closing day (December 4), they passed the document in its entirety by a vote of 2,147 to 4. The Pope promulgated it that day (that is, declared it to be the law of the Church). Then, on January 25, 1964, he said that it would come into full force on the first Sunday of Lent, February 16, 1964.

And it did.

Do you think studying a Church document can be an interesting experience? It ought to be, one should imagine. The reason is that it's all about real people and their hungers and thirsts. The Constitution of the United States can be dry-as-dust until you learn that it is the chief protection and refuge for a Jewish family that can't buy a house in a suburb heavily populated with Catholics and Protestants. The real estate men worked out a nice "restrictive covenant" clause that's all tied in with the fact that St. Malachy's Parish has a school. The priests didn't lift a finger to do any scheming—but that's not much comfort when your name is Rubin and no one will sell.

It's very much the same with the *Constitution on the Sacred Liturgy*. To be sure, it is a theological document that is 12,000 words long. It worries about matters like the parts of the divine office monks have to recite, and how priests are to celebrate Mass if they live together at a high school or college. There are some things in it that the ordinary reader won't have an immediate, lively interest in.

By and large, though, the *Constitution on the Sacred Liturgy* is concerned with big, important things: why Mississippi sharecroppers don't become Catholics (too "hard" a religion; all in a foreign language; no "gospel preaching"); why presenting Christ in Asia and Africa has such an uphill road ("a white man's religion; no appreciation of our customs"); why the laboring classes are going Marxist ("Christianity is superstitious; class-conscious; not scientific"); why the educated class in every country, including our own, stops believing in religion, by and large, or at least stops practicing it ("no intellectual satisfaction; unrelated to the needs of our age").

The Council fathers really care about these matters. They wrote all their concerns into a very realistic document.

It can come to mean something in our lives only if we study *with equal care* what they want us to do to help in Christ's work of saving the world.

2. Change in the Church: How and Why

On April 24, 1964, the newspapers had a wire-service story from Rome which said that, beginning the next day, the feast of St. Mark, priests of the Western Church should say *"Corpus Christi"* (or, subsequently, however you say "The Body of Christ" in the modern languages) as they placed the eucharist in people's mouths. The communicants were to say in response, "Amen." Now, that represents an instantaneous change in Church practice after many, many centuries of using a different prayer on this occasion.

Something similar took place during the first session of the Council in 1962 when Pope John announced that overnight St. Joseph's name was to be placed in the canon or central prayer of the Mass. Joseph was to be mentioned after our Lady and before the apostles.

We are getting used to swift-moving changes in the Church because there have been so many of them lately. Ten or twelve years ago, however, when Mass in the evening was first authorized on a Church-wide basis and the fasting rules for communion were changed, many Catholics were taken off guard. They thought these matters would never be altered, or that change would come, if at all, only after a long, slow process of discussion and debate. Then they picked up the paper one morning and learned they were wrong. Pope Pius XII had "made history" once more.

Not everyone favors change. The usual reason those who resist it do so is that they don't know why things have been as they are, or why it is now being proposed they should be another way.

Insecurity is the basic reason why people are against things. A special type of the insecure decided long ago, for example, that the command to love God and neighbor and the precepts about Sunday Mass and Friday abstinence were all equally important (offense against each being described as a "mortal sin"). They were wrong, of course, but when one card is loosened in the structure of people such as this, the whole house of cards comes down.

Being sure of things that are wrong provides the biggest insecurity of all.

Lots of people are that way about all sorts of matters: their job, school life, ways of transportation, politics, parish life.

"No, sir, not me. I'm too old to change." That means, "I'm twenty-eight and hardheaded"—or forty-eight and hardheaded. You can change the age but you have to leave the adjective the same. Doing things differently comprises a real threat to the peace and security of half the human race.

The only trouble is, *not* doing things differently comprises a threat to the whole human race. Even in religious matters that's a fact. Let's look into the question a bit.

When everyone in the Church was Jewish, in the time of the apostles, you didn't have to explain to them the notion of a sacred meal which stood for God's deliverance of His people. They had the Passover. They broke bread together, they drank ritual cups of wine, after a prayer of thanks had been spoken over their food by the father of the family.

The bread and wine as a remembrance-meal of God's deliverance through the death and resurrection of His Son was easy for the Jewish Christians. It was their Passover meal extended, fulfilled. Only now, *Jesus* was at the center of things as they made their way to God. It was no longer Moses, the lawgiver, or the patriarchs Abraham, Isaac, and Jacob, who were the chief mediators. The sacrifice of goats and lambs and heifers by priests was no longer the sign of the people's deepest interior dispositions. Now it was the man Jesus, offered once for all.

When Jews grew few in the Church, however, and Greeks grew many, there was the necessity of a *change*. It had to be explained to people who didn't have any observances quite like this what kind of meal this sacrificial eucharist was.

After three or four hundred years, the language of Rome won out. By that time most of the Christians in Europe and

Africa had ceased speaking Greek (the language in which the first generation of European Christians prayed). Actually, the tongue in use was that proper to the province of Latium, and the tribe that first spoke it was called the Latini. The point is that the liturgy had become incomprehensible to the people, and something had to be done.

You've guessed it. More *change!*

The worship of Christians at Mass and the other sacraments went into Latin, by now the "vernacular" language or that spoken by the greatest number of people in the West.

That seems reasonable enough. Religion isn't mumbo-jumbo. It is a conversation between God and His people in which by His word He gives them light and strength and they promise to serve Him forever. He does not change, but His people's customs and habits do.

What would happen if the great signs used in prayer *besides* words were to lose their meaning for people? Would the Church, at that point, change them as well? Some matters she would change, and some she wouldn't.

Take first the chief things, like bread and wine; or oil; or water.

The Church's answer on these is that she does not claim the power to do differently than the Master in the central signs He chose. There will always be baptism with water, anointing with oil, the Lord's supper in bread and wine (though all that "bread and wine" can mean it is for the centuries to decide).

When it comes to signs that the Church has made up, however, she can always change them. This extends even to the words of the sacraments. The Church can leave off using prayers, processions, gestures, and objects (like salt, or breathing on a person's forehead) any time these words or actions stop saying things to people. She can devise new signs any time she discovers that the old ones aren't saying much to people.

Our Western forms of bodily contact—for example, the kiss of peace, the saliva on a baby's tongue, the bishop's palm extended to the cheek—are repulsive to Orientals, not to speak of their having become quite meaningless by now to most men of the West. Those who try to preach the gospel in the Orient find they have a hard time of it because Christianity presents itself as a "foreign" religion. There is the further tragedy that it has, through the passage of time, become foreign to those in the very culture where it arose.

But, of course, Christianity can't really be foreign anywhere. It's not a way of life proper to Europeans, nor to white men, nor to people who speak languages derived from Latin. No. Christianity is proper to men.

That means that the one unchanging note of Christianity will always be *change*.

All of these things were much better said on the floor of the Second Vatican Council in its first session (1962) and incorporated into the *Constitution on the Sacred Liturgy* in its second session (1963). Jesus, the Master, had said that "the Sabbath was made for man, and not man for the Sabbath." (Mk. 2, 27) In other words, no single human way of doing things is to take the place of God's concern for the welfare of men—in the example Jesus chose, not even the sacred day on which God the Creator "rested."

The Council fathers said that the goal of their meeting was fourfold: to make Christian life more intense, to adapt the ways men do things to the needs of the times, to work for the religious unity of all men, and to spread the gospel. The reforms they propose to make in the liturgical rites have the same fourfold purpose as the Council itself. The very condition of meeting sinful man's perennial needs everywhere is change.

What are some of the changes that have been initially proposed? Well, things like these:

Saying *much* of the Mass in the living languages of the people, at least for the time being; it is anticipated that before long the whole Mass rite will be in people's familiar speech.

Celebrating *all* the sacraments and *all* the blessings of the Church, and reading the divine office, in living language.

Celebrating Mass in new ways (actually very old ways) which will help make the action of the Mass meaningful to everybody, like singing hymns and psalms and other chants, having readers proclaim the Scriptures and commentators give deeper meaning to the action, changing from a passive, kneeling posture to more movement and standing.

Within the near future, changing the rites of the Mass and all the sacraments notably, so that they will be more meaning-

ful to Christian people (a *consilium* or commission of forty
pastors and scholars, all but ten of them bishops, is at work
on this now).

Asking the Holy See (through national groups of bishops)
to do things *quite* differently if the customs of a people are
entirely different from those of the tenth-century West. This
will require great scholarship in ethnology and folkways, but
in a sense it is the chief thing at issue. You see, the Council's
commission is only reforming the present Roman rite. It feels
no call to create new ones.

Finally, doing certain things on one's own as a nation and
sending it off to Rome for confirmation—even within the general outlines of the Roman rite—instead of having everything
connected with sacramental prayer originate in Rome.

This last is, perhaps, the biggest change brought about
through the *Constitution on the Sacred Liturgy*. It reasserts the
principle of the decentralization of the Church for the good of
the whole Church.

The *Constitution on the Church* makes this matter explicit:
". . . Various Churches . . . have in the course of time
coalesced into several groups, organically united, which . . .
enjoy their own discipline, their own liturgical usage, and
their own theological and spiritual heritage. . . . This variety of local Churches . . . is splendid evidence of the catholicity of the one, undivided Church. In like manner, the epis-
copal bodies of today are in position to render manifold and
fruitful assistance, so that this collegiate experience may find
practical application." (Article 24) ". . . Bishops have the
sacred right and the duty before the Lord to make laws for
their subjects . . . to moderate everything pertaining to the
ordering of worship. . . . Nor are they to be regarded as
vicars of the Roman pontiffs, for they exercise an authority
that is proper to them. . . ." (Article 27)

Now, these are ancient principles of spiritual authority in
the Church. It is the return to them in practice—the Roman
pontiff's supremacy remaining unchallenged—which constitutes
the most important change of all.

3. Educating for Change – Priests and Parishioners

Once there was a tribe of primitive men who lived far up-river in the jungle, and who began to die in great numbers from the disease known as typhus. A health officer from the central government of the vast territory came to visit them. He shortly suspected the trouble, ran some tests with his field equipment, and then began to take the normal precautions.

Calling the paramount chief and the head men together, he gave strict instructions that from now on all the drinking water was to be boiled. He even gave a demonstration in the village square, where the most important business was carried on, of how this was to be done. Then he told the leaders to spread the word to all the heads of families and the women-folk. That night he rested easy for the first time in weeks.

The next day, seven more tribesmen were reported dead; the day after that, four; the third day, nine. The reason: no one was boiling his drinking water according to instructions. The doctor fumed. He pleaded. He threatened to bring the governor. He cried. Still, no one would boil any water.

You see, neither their fathers nor their fathers' fathers before them had ever boiled water. Their way, therefore, *had* to be right, and the health officer's way wrong. It was as simple as that.

That is a tale of simple folk, you may say. It couldn't happen here. The sad fact is, though, that some of the local tribesmen are college graduates and a few have even completed seminary courses. They would not think of singing lustily at Mass or walking in procession or looking straight in a fellow-parishioner's eyes, even if their lives depended on it.

Funny thing. It does.

Eternal life hinges on our participation in the mystery of Christ's death and resurrection. The chief sign of this mystery —the "mystery of faith," as the prayer over the wine calls it—

is the eucharist. A bishop leads in celebrating the eucharist in his diocese, and under his spiritual headship a pastor or the priests who assist him lead worshipers in celebrating the eucharist in parishes. The life that Christ won for us by dying and rising, the life that He holds out to us, is ours on condition that we take part in this mystery of faith.

Now, "take part in" is a phrase you can read two ways. Catholic people have been at Mass for centuries in a spirit of faith (more, or less, faith depending on the individuals) adoring the body of the Lord when it was held aloft, receiving it at communion time. That is a real participation in the Mass. It seemed to be sufficient for the needs of the times, though of course it never was. Nowadays, however, the pace of life changes. The number of things that tend to weaken faith becomes greater. A new and different participation in the Mass —in the spirit of the ancient one, in fact—is required if the deed which our Lord did on Mount Calvary is to have any lasting effect in our lives.

For all these reasons the Council fathers of Vatican II have proposed a world-wide program of popular education in the deeper meaning of the Mass. The Mass is, of course, at the center of the prayer life of the Church, like the sun in the universe. That means that no sacrament or blessing or Bible reading or prayer will go untouched by this program of renewal, for they are like planets and satellites around this sun.

"World-wide" is the adjective we used, even though the Western rites of Christendom are the only ones immediately affected; that is, those that use Latin. Still, all the Eastern patriarchs (a title higher than cardinal—the pope is the Western patriarch, for Catholics), and bishops debated these changes and voted on them at the Council, along with their Western brothers. They did so because the changes in the Roman rite will have considerable impact on the understanding the Christians of the East have of the same sacred mysteries.

Wouldn't it be tragic if the Council fathers and the experts in pastoral liturgy who advise them were like the health officer in the tropics: learned, correct in their diagnosis, men of action—yet unable to get anyone to act?

The *Constitution* drawn up at Vatican II—in force now since February 16, 1964—says that pastors need to be "thoroughly imbued with the spirit and power of the liturgy." (Article 14)

The Church's chief pastors, of course, are the bishops themselves. They received the beginnings of a marvelous formation in the liturgy through the Council's first two sessions, and they can continue in this direction by celebrating Mass and confirming and ordaining with the full, active participation of their people everywhere they go.

The bishops conducted conferences for their priests all last year, and hopefully will for years to come, at which they sat with them and listened attentively to persons especially skilled in questions of liturgical celebration and its contemplative prayer. National and regional "liturgical weeks" with bishops attending in force are the logical follow-ups. The real proof of a bishop's conviction on this matter comes when he vests for Mass and leads his priests and people in a reverent, jubilant celebration of the kind he wants to see in every parish in his diocese.

Why should bishops, who are the chief pastors, and local priests, the lesser pastors, need such formation in "the spirit and power of the liturgy"? Haven't they had years of training in all these matters in seminaries and universities?

Well, yes and no.

You see, the full spirit of understanding of the mysteries we celebrate has been dormant in the West, like a sleeping bear. One could receive a full-scale priestly education and have a reasonably effective priestly ministry *without* being well-grounded in the Bible or in a full-blown theology of the sacraments or in pastoral liturgy. It is the latter which puts the first two Christian treasures in the possession of Everyman. That possibility of non-mastery of pastoral liturgy by priests is a shame to admit, but it's true.

In order to correct things at the root, the *Constitution on the Sacred Liturgy* requires that from now on seminaries must look on liturgy as a major study, not a minor one. Instead of teaching the doctrine of the Church (dogmatic theology), ways to help people resolve their consciences (moral theology), the meaning of the Bible (sacred Scripture), and the laws of the Church (canon law) *apart* from the celebration of the sacraments, seminary professors must now attempt to give all their teaching *in conjunction with* the liturgy. "Other professors [than those who teach the history and spirit of the liturgy], while striving to expound the mystery of Christ and the history of salvation from the angle proper to each of their own subjects, must nevertheless do so in a way which will clearly bring out the connection between their subjects and the liturgy, as also the unity which underlies all priestly training." (Article 16)

The place where all this is brought together is, of course, the seminary chapel. These chapels need very much to resemble lively parish churches. Often they have been either like Friends' meetinghouses—not a bad thing in itself, but not at Mass!—or monasteries, where the liturgy is carried on beautifully provided you know all about its meaning beforehand from three dozen books. Seminaries now have to be great, vibrant centers of pastoral liturgical celebration, where it would be enjoyable for even children to go to Mass on Sunday.

If the young men studying for the priesthood began to understand the full meaning of Christ's action in the sacraments, who can tell where it might end? One thing sure is that the motherhouses where religious brothers and sisters are formed would begin to come alive in their grasp of the power of the liturgy. Yet that has begun to happen already—even earlier than in the seminaries, by and large. The colleges are beginning to feel the impact. Some Catholic colleges and Newman centers are already in very good condition as regards liturgical celebration—sometimes, in embarrassingly better condition than the parishes in the area. Pastors can learn much from them, since a college is of its nature a seat of learning.

Finally, and most importantly, the parishes of the country (with their schools and CCD programs, though not exclusively *through* them), are beginning to sing, all together, in full-throated outcry, the praise of God in the mystery of Christ's death and resurrection.

Sing!

That's the second time that verb has appeared. You see, there is no assurance of a genuine participation in the liturgy —marked by understanding—if there is no song. The gestures and movements in the rites must say something to those who participate in worship. God's word must come through to them clearly in Scripture reading and homily. The worshipers must give an attentive hearing to the prayers of the Mass and engage in dialogue with the celebrant. Then, to show they understand and approve all they have done, or what has been done in their name, priest and people together must sing.

How long will it take for every priest and layman in the country to participate lovingly and fully in the mystery of the Mass? No one knows. It is, in any case, the same length of time as that during which programs of education must continue in dioceses, parishes, seminaries and religious houses throughout the land.

4. How All the Sacred Rites Are to Be Thoroughly Revised

There is a professional class of men devoted to the careful restoration of works of art. Centuries of dust and grime settle on paintings, frescoes, and pieces of sculpture whether wood, metal, or stone. It is the work of the restorers to show them forth in their original beauty without destroying anything of the artist's touch. The unwelcome additions of time must be removed without any harm coming to the underlying work of genius.

What can happen to a work of art visible to the eye can take place in other human art forms as well. The way the Church prays publicly is one of these ways of human art.

The liturgy is made up of certain elements instituted by Christ and His Church which cannot change, and other elements which are subject to change. The Council fathers say quite unmistakably of the latter in their *Constitution on the Sacred Liturgy:* "These not only may but ought to be changed with the passage of time if they have suffered from the intrusion of anything out of harmony with the inner nature of the liturgy or have become unsuited to it." (Article 21)

What kinds of things are "out of harmony with the inner nature of the liturgy"? Chiefly, those words and actions which do little or nothing to get across to the worshipers the mystery which lies behind them.

Take an example. In the Mass of the Roman rite which most of us pray, the great "sign" is the preface-canon. It is a prayerful formula of words composed by the Church, at the heart of which are Jesus' words at the last supper, spoken over bread and wine. This entire prayer brings about the change from ordinary food to sacred food. It makes the mystery of our redemption a reality in our midst. The only trouble is, you cannot know that just from being at Mass.

The "sign-power" of words is that they convey meaning to the listener. When, in the case of the preface-canon, they are spoken silently and in a language the people cannot follow, they have their effect, all right (the bread and wine are changed), but not in the way that words are usually effective. Words are meant to affect people, not food. The change in foodstuffs comes about at the Mass through the faith the worshipers have in this mystery. Christ is faithful to His pledged word if people will have faith in Him. The faith of the Church, of priests and people alike, in the promise of Christ is what makes the preface-canon a reality. Most people present, however, have this faith, and grow in it, from some source other than the sign itself. Something else like seeing, or reading a missal, must substitute for hearing. But this is "out of harmony with the inner nature of the liturgy."

It is much the same with a baptism, a priestly ordination, or the dedication of a church, if it is celebrated in Latin or Church Slavonic. If you hold a translation in your hand you get some of the meaning of the sacred rite. The learned few may not need a translation if their hearing and the priest's diction are both good. Still, there are many times when you may know the meaning of all the prayers and even then they won't "say anything to you." There is something coming between you and the tongue in which you think and speak—and dream at night!

In sixth-century Rome, the priest did thus and so with his hands. The people got the message. That gesture *always* meant such-and-such to them.

Nowadays, he performs the same action in Lackawanna, New York, or La Cañada, California, and it doesn't say a thing to the worshipers. Some people have missals which explain why the priest does this action, and the missals will be wrong! The sixth-century Romans would throw back their heads and laugh at the explanation given. Why? Because the missal author is a bad scholar who simply doesn't know the right reasons for things. And some sacred rites are so obscure by now that not even the best scholars are sure what they meant originally.

"In this restoration," the document directs, "both texts and rites should be drawn up so that they express more clearly the holy things which they signify; the Christian people, so far as possible, should be enabled to understand them with ease and to take part in them fully, actively, and as befits a community." (Article 21)

We are still a long way from that. Will we ever be able to close in the gap?

The men whom Pope Paul has named to take the first step in doing it are the forty members of the commission for follow-up (*"ad exsequendam"*) on the sacred liturgy. We have mentioned that they are bishops, chiefly (and a few priests), from all over the globe. Many of them were the best discussants of the worship question during the Council itself. They are being assisted by scholarly experts, just as the bishops were before and during the Council. Good numbers among them have a well-developed pastoral sense, a feeling for people's possibilities and needs. It is the members of this commission, together with the Sacred Congregation of Rites, whom the Pope has empowered to act for him in confirming the decrees which the bishops of the various countries send him authorizing changes in the language of the liturgy.

They will act for him, too, when national groups of bishops say they want more of the Mass in their people's mother tongues than the *Constitution* spells out—or all of the Mass in their mother tongue, if that is their wish. Most importantly, though, the members and consultors of both commission and congregation are at work now recasting the rites of all the sacraments and other public prayers of the Church of the West. They got the word to do this, remember, from all the bishops of Christendom who are in communion with Rome, East and West.

"The liturgical books are to be revised as soon as possible; experts are to be employed on the task, and bishops are to be consulted, from various parts of the world." (Article 25)

The commission members have been given a good set of directives for their task. They are not left strictly on their own, in other words. The rites should be simple, says the *Constitution*—short, clear, and not weighed down with useless repetitions. (See Article 34.) Some examples of the latter would be the many signs of the cross at Mass (of which a few were eliminated March 7, 1965), the still-remaining double "Lord, I am not worthy," or the multiple prayers to drive out Satan in the rite of baptism. Everything that is done in the liturgy "should be within the people's power of comprehension, and normally should not require much explanation." (Article 34)

Suppose the members of the commission work out something that everybody in Lackawanna and La Cañada can comprehend just by being present at in a spirit of faith with open eyes and ears (an unlikely proposition—the ancient Roman approach to prayer was *very* different—but let's suppose it). Anyway, the commission then sends the revised rites off to Utsunomiya or Tonga. They are dutifully translated by scholars in those parts. The Japanese people, and the Tanzanians, say, "I can understand the words in my own language, but what are all those funny movements? Nobody here acts *that* way, least of all when he's trying to pray." Klunk! A dead end. The "intimate connection between words and rites" (Article 35) is not apparent in the liturgy, at least not in downtown Tonga or suburban Utsunomiya. What then?

"Provisions shall also be made, when revising the liturgical books, for legitimate variations and adaptations to different groups, regions, and peoples, especially in mission lands. . . . In some places and circumstances, however, an even more radical adaptation of the liturgy is needed. . . . Elements from the traditions and culture of individual peoples might then appropriately be admitted into divine worship." (Articles 38, 40)

Many people don't come to church, not because they don't have faith in God, but because church is so "churchy." It doesn't say a *thing* to them. It isn't part of life as they know it.

The whole Church in Council has said: "Precisely!" The present-day prayer forms of all seven sacraments are full of details, large and small, that are out of harmony with the inner nature of liturgy.

Signs—including words—are meant to signify. When they don't, and in the liturgy in its present state they frequently don't, the Church has said, "They've *got* to go!"

5. How Long Is an Interim?

During World War II, when lots of things were in short supply and the amount of recreation, travel, and ordinary *eating* people could do was severely cut down, you saw signs all over saying, "Closed for the Duration." It got so that people asked after a while, "I wonder how long the duration will last?"

We can ask the same question about the length of the interim period between the first use of English speech in the Mass liturgy (November 29, 1964, in the United States) and the final revised form of the Mass and the remaining sacraments. After the work-teams in Rome and then in the various countries of the world have recast them, the rites should really say something to people. With that, we ought to have the end of the interim period. How far off is that?

"Interim" is a Latin adverb that can be translated "meanwhile." But a meanwhile is a medium-while or middle-while, a space of time between. Between what? In the case of the liturgy, between a first reform and a final reform: final for now, that is, for in a hundred years or so the whole matter will need looking into again. That, of course, is what hasn't been happening in the Western Church for the last four hundred years. That is why a council was so desperately needed—to deal with this matter along with so many others.

We've spoken earlier of how touchy people are about things that affect their Christian lives. You can make changes in advertising, in education, and even in political structures much more readily than you can in the way people pray.

The reason is that God is Someone sure; He is certain; He is there. When you change the ways in which we speak to Him, people have the general uneasy feeling that this may be calling into question the fact that He is unchanging; that He is certain; that He is there.

Our recent popes have done a lot to teach us the difference

between an unchanging Catholic faith and constantly improved ways of expressing it. Pope Pius XII (1939–1958) was a great figure in this regard. He helped us change our way of thinking about all sorts of matters: the Bible, the Church, the liturgy, war and peace, technology. If he had defects (and his whole public conduct during the war is under severe scrutiny) they were a result of his commitment from youth to the channels of diplomacy, his being a prisoner of *Romanità.* But his pastoral instincts were all good.

After him came Pope John XXIII (1958–1963) who reminded us how out of touch Church life was with all sorts of things that real people experience and do. He took lots of stodginess and downright bluff out of "official" religious life and looked things squarely in the eye. His last great letter, *Peace on Earth,* is miles away from the usual content and tone of a papal encyclical. It calls a spade a spade, not a horticultural instrument.

The ground has been prepared in any number of ways (to continue that figure of speech) for the possibility of a fairly quick changeover to new and better patterns of public prayer. Below are some of the steps on the way to the "end of the interim."

Bishops and superiors of religious orders of priests need to work unremittingly at in-service training for the clergy. The people simply can't pray better publicly than the opportunities that are held out to them. There have to be meetings and seminars and demonstrations of every sort. Many priests need to learn for the first time what it means to be a public figure presiding over a community action at the Mass, at a baptism, a wedding, or a funeral. The sad fact is that the liturgy has become a private prayer for all of us, even for priests. But of its nature it is a common celebration, a joint venture.

The whole Catholic body needs to become very familiar with the Bible. Actually, the inner meaning of the Church's prayer through sacraments and sacramentals is available to us only if we are soaked in the Scriptures.

There must be a conviction as widespread as the Church itself that choral song by the whole congregation is a Christian good. Choirs, choirmasters, and organists, above all, need to be convinced that this is true, that they are the great friends to people's song and it to them, not that they are great enemies.

Lastly, all who teach in the Church, whether it be parents, catechists, journalists, or anyone else who instructs in a formal way, need to see how central the liturgy is in the Church's apostolate of total Christian formation. Schools, Confraternity classes, and homes do a work that leads up to the work the Church does when she prays commonly. If the catechism class doesn't see itself as out on the edges of the work of religious education, and the Mass or Bible service as in at the center, nothing really good can come of the total program, for the terms will be wrong.

Well, that's quite a lot to require for the interim period, isn't it? The whole thing sounds like "Open End." We'll be old, old men before we see that happening, many must be thinking.

It's much easier to name certain target dates, or guess at them, than speculate on when the whole job of reform will be done. For example: by November 29, 1964, all the parishes in the United States had begun to pray the portions of the Mass in the official interim missal in English. By March 7, 1965, the commission on follow-up of the *Constitution* told us that the "liturgy of the word," that is, the early instructional part of the Mass, was to be celebrated away from the altar. On such and such a date in 1967 (what year is anybody's guess) the revised Roman rite of the Mass will be available—following which national groups of bishops will then begin to ask for departures even from that to meet the special needs of their people.

It is easy to name the factors that could bring various interim periods to an end, if we simply concentrated on Church law or requirement.

Those kinds of interims are deceitful, though. They are never really over. The dates for "shaping up" just mark the beginning of new hurt feelings for some, while others are delighted with the improved pattern of celebration the advent of a certain date requires.

The only target date worth working and praying for is that

at which the liturgy will produce its full effects, "the faithful [and priests] coming to it with proper dispositions, their minds attuned to their voices." (Article 11) And when that happy day will be . . . knows God!

6. Public Prayer – or Private Prayer Said Publicly?

The reason a symphony orchestra has a conductor is that the hundred or so musicians, despite their considerable skill, could very well slip into disunity unless someone was constantly helping them play as one.

A base-path coach in baseball has a similar function. The runner can't look in all directions; he's much too close to the action. The coach, therefore, acts as eyes and ears for him.

The cast in a stage play, the members of a sports team, and the ground crew at an airfield are all persons who work together to accomplish a single objective. If anyone fails to do his job there will be trouble. The joint venture just won't work.

No one complains that a symphony conductor or the leading man in a play was visible throughout the evening. That's his job. You don't mind not seeing the orchestra's booking agent or the play's stage manager. But with the leading figure in an evening of music or drama, either he exercises his function publicly or else there is no performance.

That's the way it is when the Church prays her liturgy. You can stand it if the sacristan isn't in full view or the women who bake the altar breads. Without a congregation of people, however, or a priest and servers, without a commentator and a director of song, you haven't got the necessary elements for the liturgy. Oh, a priest and an altar boy can "go it alone." There's no question as to whether the thing is possible. We say, in defense of this arrangement, "The whole Church is with them in spirit." Still, the liturgy is by nature a public function. It is something done by people: real people who are there, not imaginary people who couldn't make it that morning.

The priest (best of all, the bishop) who "celebrates" the liturgy really does that. He is in charge of a genuine public celebration. On weekdays it may be a fairly subdued affair, but at all times it is a public happening. If the priest is so far away he can't be seen, or can be seen but can't be heard, he will be that much less effective with the people he is leading.

Catholic people don't like exaggeration, flamboyant behavior in their celebrants. Still, they appreciate a priest who really leads them in a public act. The soft-voiced celebrant who drones the Mass or the prayers of anointing of the sick may be a very pious person immersed in prayer, but he's practically useless for the job he was ordained for.

That's a pretty strong statement, but it's true. He was given the task of leading the Church in prayer, and all he's doing is praying privately in full view of certain of her members. The fact that he's doing it in Christ's name and in theirs is the only thing that justifies his performance.

Well, isn't that enough?

No, that isn't enough.

Next question.

The next question is a long and complicated one. How is it that the liturgy became such a private affair, if by nature it was never intended to be that? Well, the language problem had a lot to do with it. If you are speaking words to people who can't understand you, the incentive to say them "loud and clear" drops to the zero point—especially if your back is toward them. That, in fact, is exactly what happened in the case of many priests, even the most zealous ones.

Four centuries ago, at the last official reform of the missal, the celebrant was instructed to say certain things in an audible tone (such as the Scripture readings). The most important prayer of all, the canon of the Mass, he was told to say inaudibly. This gave official sanction to the idea that the Mass is of its nature a private prayer.

The notion is wrong, of course, but all sorts of wrong ideas had led up to it. The altar, for example, had for centuries been traveling away from the people toward the back wall of the church. It was even put behind a partition or screen which made the sacred enclosure invisible. This is called a rood screen in the West, an *ikonóstasis* (picture-wall) in the East. There were great domes built on churches, and directly under them was placed—nothing! The action of Christ and His people had retreated deep into the area where the choir should be; rather, Christ and His priest had gone traveling, and His people were left gaping behind, possessing Him—barely—by remote control.

In big churches it made no sense for the ministers of the liturgy to act as if they were in charge of the public prayer of the congregation. The communication lines had been cut. The clergy and servers were in charge of themselves. The result was that the plays at the altar became more and more complicated: T-formations with the censer, single-wing backs with the "boat." We're not making fun. That's exactly what happened. If you've ever been to a pontifical Mass, old-style, you'll know what we mean.

There have been several serious results of all this and they've been building up for hundreds of years. One is that some masters of ceremonies are having a very hard time, emotionally, seeing why it is that the liturgy is an action of the people. For them, just as for a ballet master, it was always an affair of the troupe, the performers. Choirmasters and organists are in the same condition, by and large. They say they want to preserve good music in church, and that's fine, but subconsciously many of them believe that unskilled labor has begun to apply. The *people* want to sing the people's parts ("Lord, have mercy"; "Glory to God"; etc.), and that's something many choirmasters and organists have never experienced! After a very brief experience of it they decide they don't like it. With all sorts of proper parts and motets to perform, and the congregation to sustain, they decide nonetheless that "There's nothing left for the choir to do."

The priests are none too happy either. They had been taught to cast their eyes down when they faced the people to address them (at *"Dominus vobiscum,"* etc.), to mumble away softly at the most important moments, in a word, not to "distract" the people by looking human up there, let alone by leading them actively in what they were doing.

By all odds, though, it is the people we should pity most in the restoration of the true idea of liturgy. For years they had been conditioned to skip the high Mass, that deadly performance. Now something very much like it is to be found at almost any hour they pick. They are being asked to "bob up and down," as they put it. They are being pressed to sing. They are complaining that they're being "bothered" at Mass. Why can't they be let alone to "pray"?

Actually, the psychological condition of all concerned is very delicate. You see, the changeover is a basic one for all: from private meditation to public participation. This is going to be hard on everybody—until a certain magic moment arrives in the life of each one, and of course it will happen singly. That moment is the point of realization on the part of individuals that we haven't really had the mystery of the Mass right at all. It is meant to be a great public act, something you do *as a people,* not just something you do in the company of other people. There is an invisible line, as it were, which people cross over once they discover what kind of prayer the Mass is meant to be.

The "new liturgy" is an absolute reversal of thought which takes us back to things as they are. This public prayer of God's people is, indeed, the only liturgy the Church has ever had. There has been a Rip Van Winkle snooze of a thousand years, that's all. But the liturgy is emerging now, like the sun from behind the clouds. Like a giant it is "joyfully running its course . . . from one end of the sky to the other." (Ps. 18 [19], 6f.)

Catholics have discovered prayer, in its most classic form. They may stumble on Christianity next!

7. The Deed of God that Saves Us

The cornerstone of our faith is that God is present in the world to sanctify and save it. We believe not simply in *God*, but in God as He acts to bring us Himself. The way He does this is by taking an active part in our earthly, human lives.

God's activity in our behalf is a continuing thing. It is a thing of now. We are quite right to ask God in our prayers, as the old joke says the voter asked the politician, "Yes, but what have you done for me lately?"

That is why we would be quite wrong if we supposed that the liturgy is one big harking back to the past, an exercise in "far away and long ago." It is nothing of the sort. The unfortunate fact is that since the vestments we use are out of the past, and the Latin language is out of the past, and the prayers and bodily movements are out of the past, the whole performance may seem outdated. We who pray the liturgy might be prone to think that we are merely making present an event out of the past.

We who celebrate the Mass or any sacrament as a holy community—as a Christian people—are doing something in the present that stands for something else that is going on in the present. It is true that it has important reference to the past. Jesus Christ is in heaven, "the holy city of Jerusalem," now, "sitting at the right hand of God." (*Constitution,* Article 8) The Council fathers, quoting the Letter to the Hebrews (8, 2), call Him "a minister of the holies and of the true tabernacle [tented sanctuary]." They say that in the preface of the Mass, just before it concludes with "Holy, Holy, Holy," we sing a concert of praise with all the heavenly army, the angels and saints who praise God at this moment.

The priest at Mass presides over a true sacrificial meal in our midst. It is the same sacrifice as the offering of praise

Christ is making *now* to His Father in the heavenly court. The fact that it is a remembrance rite or memorial of a death and resurrection that happened in the past is secondary to its importance as an event of today. In the liturgy, God is at work to sanctify and save us. "My Father has never yet ceased his work," Jesus said when He healed a man on the Sabbath, "and I am working too." (Jn. 5, 17)

We can't insist too strongly that while important things have happened in past history, the history that matters to you and me is your personal history and mine. This fact has at least two serious implications.

One is that "changes in the liturgy" are next to meaningless if they only change our ways of external behavior. A year or two ago congregations knelt silently all through the Mass in their parish churches. This year it began to be a standing and singing and lots-more-listening routine. So who cares? Normal people can only begin to care if they realize that much more is happening to them than standing, singing, and listening. That means that much more must, in reality, be happening to them. If they get to the point where they know that Christ is working for them in this action now, just as His Father does, then they'll *really* begin to care.

This is, in point of fact, what God has done for us lately.

The second important thing implied by the fact of "action now" in the liturgy is that modern history—yours and mine— has a special importance because of what God has done in the past to save all men.

When He made the world out of His abounding love, there was the beginning of history. A foaming crater—a swirling ocean of billions of tons—no one around to appreciate either; only a few squirming creatures working their way up to be fishes and birds, beasts and men. But already "sacred history" had begun. God makes history holy because He is holy. He, the Holy One, is the world's creator and fashioner. When He initiates history it is holy by that very fact.

When God makes men in His image and likeness we have come to another stage in sacred history. Making man His special friend accompanied that first creation (theologians call this friendship "original justice"). That first bestowal of grace was, in some way, His first great breaking into human history. So great is His love for us, He did it again and again: in the call of Abraham and his whole career, in the choice of Moses, in the entire outworking of the Exodus, in the lives of all the patriarchs and the prophets. And lastly, in His Son.

The *Constitution on the Sacred Liturgy* makes a brief presentation of sacred history in its early portion. (Articles 5–10) This history is none other than the life of God with man—on this earth, in time. In our time. Men are made holy and God is given glory by what goes on in churches and in factories and on streets *now*.

The central event in sacred history—the great decisive action on God's part which divides all time into "before" and "after"—is what the *Constitution* calls "the paschal mystery of Christ." (Article 6) This mystery is "his blessed passion, resurrection from the dead, and glorious ascension, whereby 'dying, he restored our death and, rising, he restored our life.'" (Article 5)

We are freed from the power of Satan and from death, we are brought into the kingdom of the Father, if by baptism we let ourselves be plunged into this mystery: dying with Christ, being buried with Him, rising with Him. At the level of *history,* God's deed in Christ is a thing of the past. At the level of *mystery,* in the sacraments, it is a thing of the present.

The whole point of changing the language of the sacraments, reading more Scripture, having better sermons, having a deeper understanding of the ceremonies, is that we should walk into church and there meet God, then come out and encounter Him again and again in various ways. We meet Him in *our lives,* not in Moses' life or in David's life. We do not meet Him only in church, but we do meet Him there in a special way.

God's supreme deed to save us—summing up the whole history of Israel—was His acceptance of the obedient Jesus as our pleader, our brother. Jesus' life of glory, His life in the Spirit now, is grace to us. God's later deed to save us is really only the one, same deed, but this time in sign. He comes forward to meet us each time we pray the liturgy.

God is in our history, addressing us and claiming us through it. If we are His sheep we will recognize His voice. The Jesus we serve is the Messiah who is both come, and to come, in our flesh. We must get to know Him here, in our lives, where He is.

8. What Christ Does when He Prays

One comforting thing about life (where, it seems, there is all too little to comfort us), is that each person has a job to do. Some people don't get much consolation out of *that*, we must admit. A job for comfort? There is a line from *The Irish Rover* on a record cut by the Clancy Brothers and Tommy Makem which describes one of the crew members this way: "There was Paddy Joe McGurk, He was scared to death o' work . . ."

Unless you happen to be in full flight from gainful employment, you'll know about the security that comes with feeling you're needed to do a job.

You may not be sure what that job is. The thought that there is a niche for you somewhere is strength enough to go on. It helps you look for your niche, or stay at your work in life once you've found it.

If it were pointed out to you that Christ had a job to do, you'd see immediately what was meant. You'd say, "Sure, He came to die for us." That might be modified to read, "He came to die and rise for us," but there would be understanding from the start.

If it were said, however, that Christ is still at work in our behalf, you might wonder what this means, exactly. "He's God, isn't He? You just pray to Him, and He answers you in the way God answers. Isn't the phrase, 'He's working,' just playing with words?" Those questions probably speak for most Christians who give the matter any thought at all.

Here is the way the *Constitution on the Sacred Liturgy* speaks of the work of Jesus, both in time and eternity (Article 5). First, He came in "the fullness of time," this Son of God who is the Word made flesh. This means when God thought the world was ready for Him, or at the time His work could have its best effect.

The Lord Jesus was "anointed by the Holy Spirit, to preach the gospel to the poor, to heal the contrite of heart." The Council fathers are quoting the Book of Isaiah (61, 1) and the gospel according to Luke (4, 18) in that description of our Lord's work. Anointing by the Holy Spirit meant that the man Jesus was God-filled and God-directed in all that He did.

St. Ignatius of Antioch, martyred about eighty years after the resurrection, says that the Word became one of us to be a "bodily and spiritual medicine" to us. *He is also the mediator between God and man.*

Now, what does that word "mediator" mean? Middleman, quite simply. How is He the middleman? In the sense that "His humanity, united with the person of the Word, was the instrument of our salvation." (Article 5) God saved us men through the human mind and emotions of one of us, through the eyes, ears, heart, and tongue of Jesus of Nazareth. What one man did was effective in behalf of all the rest. He was "the perfect achievement of our reconciliation." (*Ibid.*) In other words, man was not in the least set against God in the person of Christ. He was a perfectly obedient human son of His heavenly Father, one who worshiped God fully in our very midst.

Was this obedience of His "work" in any strict sense? We are compelled to say that it was. Although Jesus was, in fact, the eternal Word or Son of God, this didn't relieve His human soul from challenge or pain. If you and I find it hard to live in the midst of people who don't pray much, or who don't love greatly, imagine how hard it must have been for Him. Obedience is hard for any man because he is sinful. Jesus became not simply man but sinful man, even though He was not Himself a sinner. He had the human condition, and it is a sinful condition. He faced life with all its humiliation, death with all its pain.

"He achieved his task principally by the paschal mystery of his blessed passion, resurrection from the dead, and glorious ascension, whereby 'dying, he destroyed our death and, rising, he restored our life.'" So says Article 5 of the liturgy constitution, quoting the Easter preface from the Roman missal.

This looks like familiar territory. What is being said in the language of the Mass is that Christ saved us by dying on the cross and coming forth from the tomb. The work of Christ is a single work; it is also over, done with. He needs to die no more. He can never emerge from the grave again for the simple reason that it is needless to do so. He is in glory.

But while Christ is with His Father and all the saints, He is not apathetic. He is forever active. He prays. This doesn't mean, of course, that He is on His knees or busy about making up prayers. No, it means that Jesus' human will is fixed on two things: giving God glory, and remembering you and me in our needs. To accomplish this, the only requirement is that He should be with His Father. His presence in heaven suffices to have Him praise God and intercede for us. The prayers of the Mass make this clear, chiefly the canon. The other "ordinary" prayers do this as well, and likewise the "proper" ones which change from Mass to Mass.

The Christian people give the Almighty Father "all honor and glory, in Him, with Him, and through Him" who is Christ the Lord. This goes on continuously, from the fact that "Christ is always present in his Church, especially in her liturgical celebrations." (Article 7) The heavenly liturgy continues unabated so that the needy on earth may derive profit from it. Praise is its first motive, but intercession is its second.

Every time we come to Mass or baptize a baby or anoint a sick person, Jesus Christ "exercises his priestly office." (Article 7) In other words, He is active in His Church to save us, its members, by being active in heavenly prayer. He acts as a middleman in our behalf, presenting our needs and awaiting the Father's action of grace.

No other action the Church engages in can rival in effectiveness the sanctification of men through sacramental signs. The senses take in the fact that the whole mystical body, Jesus Christ the head and all who are with Him in faith, is worshiping God. This is the way we know that Christ is praying for us.

He left behind Him ways for us to pray in signs, with the guarantee that He would be praying to His Father at the same time and that the two prayers would be one.

We always seem to come to the same conclusion in these

pages, no matter where we start. Let us flush it out of the thicket this time with a question or two.

"How do we know that Christ is at prayer in the liturgy? Is it because someone says so?"

Not at all. We know it from the liturgy itself (presuming we have Christian faith to start with).

"But what if the liturgy tells us nothing about what Christ does when He prays?"

Then, it is badly celebrated. Even when it is well celebrated in its present condition, however, it is not easy to know what Christ is busy about. Then is it proved all the more—on the occasion of a flawless public celebration—how much the liturgy needs to be reformed!

9. The Word of God Proclaimed to Men

If God is mute, He is quite meaningless to us.

Unless He *can* speak, and in fact *does* speak, it doesn't much matter whether He "exists" or not (that famous question from apologetics classes).

Should "God" be merely a human word to describe a dull blur beyond the clouds, it doesn't make a great deal of sense to spend a lifetime trying to love and serve Him.

If, however, God is a person who is all, and in all, then the great minimum we should expect of Him is that He will have something to say to us from time to time.

The only God we Christians believe in is a Father who speaks to us in recognizable accents of love. He does deeds of love in our behalf. These deeds are His words, in one sense. The written record of His deeds are His words, in another sense.

It was the same with Israel long before us, that people to whom God spoke in the events of its national history. The deliverance from Egypt was God's great word of compassion to this people. It brought them into existence as "my people." God spoke to them again and again in fragmentary and varied fashion through the prophets.

God's word to His people would take the form of a crushing defeat by Assyria, let us say. A prophet would rise up to tell the people (who had just lived through the disaster, and couldn't tell *what* it meant): "Thus says the Lord," or, "A word of the Lord to Isaiah" or whoever it might be. This "word of the Lord" would be the true meaning—God's meaning—of what had just taken place.

If a friend says to you, "Sure, I'll run you into town," you have a word from him which is, at the same time, a deed. It is plain speech, and it is the language of love. Now, why can't God speak to us as clearly as that?

The reason is that He is God and not a man. If His speech were human speech, or the next thing to it, this would plainly be unworthy of Him. After all, He is the infinite God. We cannot expect Him to converse with us and show His affection in exactly the same way as our friends do.

"In this the final age," says that early Christian who wrote the Letter to the Hebrews, "he has spoken to us in the Son whom he has made heir to the whole universe . . . the Son who is the effulgence of God's splendor and the stamp of God's very being." (Heb. 1, 2–3) That makes Jesus our Lord God's final means of communicating with us—the clearest thing He has ever had to say on who He is and who we are.

Jesus is the last word of God to men.

St. John says as much at the beginning of the fourth gospel by calling Him who became flesh as Jesus Christ, "the Word." (Jn. 1, 14) He came to dwell among us, this man of whom the Baptist testified that before he, John was born, He already was. (Jn. 1, 30) The "word of life" was the theme of all the apostolic teaching. It was a life made visible and shared in the person of Jesus Christ. (See 1 Jn. 1, 2–4.) Often the apostolic teachers spoke of this word of life as a word of salvation, a message, or tidings of which they were the servants.

They meant by this that their Master was Jesus, and that nothing would do but that they proclaim the truth about Him. He was, after all, God's final word. In Christ Jesus, man and message are one. "I became its servant [Christ's body which is the Church] by virtue of the task assigned to me by God for your benefit: to deliver his message in full; to announce the secret hidden for long ages and through many generations . . . the secret is this: Christ in you, the hope of a glory to come." (Col. 1, 25–27)

Now, if the whole point of the person of Jesus Christ is that God is coming in touch with us through Him, and if the whole point of the Church is that it brings this word of life to men, then you might say that nothing much matters except that through the Church men should hear the word of God and keep it. This is, of course, the way things are. That is why Central Catholic High exists or St. Sophia's Cathedral Sunday School or the Covenant Presbyterian school of religion. They exist to proclaim the word of God to men. If that isn't what happens there but only studies, sports, and moralizing lessons, they might as well shut up shop.

To be quite accurate, a catechetical situation does not exist to proclaim the word of God so much as to prepare for its fruitful hearing and study out its implications once it has been heard. The classic place for proclaiming God's word in human hearing is the holy assembly—chiefly the eucharistic assembly. That is where God longs to speak to men, above all, and tell them what He thinks the events in the life of His Son ought to mean in their lives. He wants to make clear what the events of their lives mean as seen through the prism of this Christ-event.

Now, the lives of normal people are filled with mystery and hardship. Children get run over on their bikes; young mothers of six children die at thirty-eight; good women don't get a husband; sin and scandal are everywhere.

When they come to church on Sunday, these people desperately need to hear the word of God proclaimed in their hearing during the assembly. If the priest just drones out announcements about the parish activities for the week, what can they mean to the man in anguish, the Christian who is feeling the pain of life—or death? God has acted in his life lately—in a terrifying way, let us suppose. What does the deed, the experience, the event *mean?* Will no true teacher in Israel tell him, neither Jesus, nor St. Paul, nor the homilist, nor the reader? If not, he may stop coming to Mass and stay away for ten or twenty years. The Church will have failed to fill the greatest need in his life: to tell him about the things that matter most to him.

Not every Sunday in people's lives is a crisis of that sort. But every Sunday is a crisis of some sort in someone's life, and the regularly recurring Masses that never speak to these situations are missing the reality of human life entirely. That is why the *Constitution on the Sacred Liturgy* insists so much that, in the worship of God, "God speaks to his people, and Christ is still proclaiming his gospel." (Article 33)

The people's response in song and in prayer to this word of God is itself no less a word of God. In fact, the whole action of the Mass and not just the early parts—epistle, gospel, hom-

ily—is a word of God to His people. What is the canon of the
Mass, that great consecratory prayer, if not a making present
to save us of Him who is the Word of life?

All of the liturgy, then, is a saving word of God to men.
This is true in a special way of "visible signs . . . prayers,
and songs" (Article 33) which are meaningful, of rites
"within the people's power of comprehension." (Article 34)
It is true of "more reading from holy Scripture, which is to be
more varied and suitable," of sermons the content of which is
drawn mainly from the Bible and the texts of the liturgy and
the people's lives. All liturgical preaching is, of its nature, a
"proclamation of God's wonderful works in the history of
salvation." (Article 35)

Can you see all that the Church envisions in a reformed
liturgy? No less than a sacred assembly in which God ceases
to be mute in the midst of His people.

10. The Difference in Sermons

John Singer Sargent, the portrait painter, is reported to have said, by way of defining his own art: "A portrait is something that is a little bit wrong around the mouth."

A rough, working definition of a sermon might be that it is, or has been at any rate, a comprehensible interlude in the Mass that congregations wait for to be over.

Consider what a sermon or homily is. (The classic type of sermon during a liturgical celebration is called a homily.) It is a further extension of the word of God which has just been proclaimed during the "liturgy of the word," namely the first and second readings. It is an exploration by the whole assembly, in a spirit of lively faith, of one point in the gospel of Jesus Christ. Often it will be a point that came up in the gospel reading of the day, but it need not be that. After all, the gospel in its entirety is rich, but those fifty-two Sunday readings are severely limited selections.

The important thing about a sermon is that the people should have had the word of God in the Scriptures proclaimed to them first. A homily flows naturally from an intelligent and fully audible reading of the inspired books of the Holy Spirit. If the case was, however, that the reading from the Old Testament or the apostle Paul was not understood by the reader, or if the day's selection from the evangelist was read out lifelessly like a much-played record, then no real extension of God's word is possible. The minimum conditions were absent from the start.

For the word of God to be fruitful, congregations must *want* to hear it. Too often they have no desire to hear the divine word. Oh, they want to hear "better preaching," they say, but that often means no more than a series of clear examples and a quick wrap-up.

Notice how often it happens that the Mass of that priest

who preaches "too long" will be skipped by parishioners, when his chief fault is that he preaches too tellingly, or indeed preaches every time he celebrates Mass. The sermon is something quite big and serious for him. It is no less than God's word! It stopped being that for some of his people years ago. Their religion has turned into a choppy, high-speed, little deal with God. Theirs is strictly a no-nonsense approach which wants its two elevations accomplished with a decent minimum of droning and no extra talk whatever. The sermon is just a waste of time for people such as these. It is that, unfortunately, for some priests.

Let's turn back to the preacher for a minute. What does he need in order to give a good homily every time he speaks to the sacred assembly? Well, he needs to love God dearly, first of all. Then he needs to love the people who are entrusted to him. They may be his just for the morning, if he is a visitor, or they may be men and women with whom he shares many years of his life. In either case, he must care for them deeply. He must worry about the fact that, in the nine or thirteen minutes at his disposal, they need bread, and he runs the risk of giving them a stone.

In other words, he needs to have great faith in the power of God's word. He must believe in it as the energizing force without which none of the seven sacraments could have its effect. Many priests have not understood the power of preaching in this way. The whole Church needs to grow to understand that the sacramental signs cannot have their full, intended effect apart from the lively faith of the believer.

But, as St. Paul points out, there is no ordinary way to faith if one has not heard of the Lord Jesus. "And how are they to hear without someone to spread the news?" (Rom. 10, 14) Spreading the news requires a commission to do so. Well, preachers have that. They need, besides, a great conviction about the importance of preaching. They must be convinced that, without good sermons, people will simply never hear God speak to them in His ordinary way in the Church.

Preaching is a high art, hence difficult for any mortal man to do. Listening to God's word is also a high art, and a great challenge to faith.

What have the fathers of the Second Vatican Council done to improve the situation in preaching? Merely pointing out what's wrong does not provide either the clergy or the people with nearly enough help in this difficult matter.

In the *Constitution on the Sacred Liturgy* the Council fathers have made it clear that "the sermon is part of the liturgical service" (Article 35), as much a part as the readying of the bread and wine, or the canon itself. A very serious reason is needed to omit the sermon on a Sunday or holy day of obligation. (See Article 52.) Priests are required to preach "with exactitude and fidelity." Careful preparation of thoughts about the gospel of Jesus Christ is called for here.

The sermon, however, is not just any prepared discourse about holy things. Its main sources are "scriptural and liturgical," in other words the record of what God has done to save man in history. "The mystery of Christ, ever made present and active within us, especially in the celebration of the liturgy" (Article 35), is what the priest is required by the *Constitution* to preach about most. That means that he has to explore with the people just how the Savior is using the signs of *this* Mass in *this* week of people's lives to bring them the grace of salvation.

One important thing going on in the Church which will help make preaching better, and hearing God's word for that matter, is that the study of Scripture is being much improved. Many priests and people are going deeper and deeper into the meaning of God's word in the Bible, which means they are exploring His total word in their lives.

A deeper knowledge of the riches of sacramental life is being made available to all through better scholarship. The liturgy, of course, first began to be celebrated in the apostolic Church. Much of the New Testament collection comes to us from the prayers and the worship of apostolic times. One needs to know the biblical books and the history of the rites very well before he can see or make clear to others how Christ is at work sanctifying through sacraments.

"By means of the homily, the mysteries of the faith and the guiding principles of the Christian life are expounded from

the sacred text, during the course of the liturgical year."
(Article 52)

Have you heard better preaching or been a party to better
listening in your parish church lately? You are going to. Nothing can stop the power of God's word, once priests and people
begin to discover the gift this word is to the whole Church.

11. The Difference in Catechisms and Religion Classes

Jesus was a very interesting teacher. He wasn't a bore. The crowds never grew tired of Him. They said, "No one ever talked to us like this before."

All of us like interesting teachers. If we happen to teach, we'd like to believe that we are interesting teachers.

What is the special gift of a good teacher? In what does his talent consist?

We talk about the good teacher's gift, but that doesn't mean we have it.

Well, an interesting teacher is someone who is interested in his students. He likes people more than he likes his subject matter. Oh, he may be all wrapped up in biology or literature. You hope he is, in fact. Some of the worst teachers we've ever had are those who have lost all interest in their subject. But the good teacher cares more about *you* than *it*, in the sense that he's very concerned that you should know what he's teaching you—you, personally, that is, all thirty-eight of you.

It's a funny thing, but some of the most interesting teachers we have don't get to know us by name. We're sure they have a personal interest in each of us, but somehow they're still trying to sort out Janice Miller and Janet Martin by the end of the year. At the other end of the scale are the teachers who know all about us but only seem interested in us on their terms, not on ours.

Good teachers don't use too many words to say a thing. They don't employ a vocabulary that's beyond us all the time (although they don't hesitate to introduce an occasional new word, which they explain). Their rate of teaching is very close to the students' rate of learning; they're not a million miles out in front of them, or seven miles behind.

The most important point of all, though, is that the good teacher always talks about things in terms of what's going on in the students' lives. Sometimes that's not easy to do, for example if there is a particular student who couldn't care less about how to convert centigrade into Fahrenheit or about the rules for the partitive in French. Still, if there's any bridge whatever from the subject matter to a student's life, *this* teacher will find a way to build it.

What was special about Jesus was that He had *all* of these good qualities and not just some of them. He really cared about His listeners, which made them really care about Him.

It would be nice to report that every Christian teacher teaches like Jesus. Alas, it is not so! Far from being the best taught subject in the curriculum, religion is often the worst. Why should this be? Well, among other reasons, because religion isn't a "subject" in the ordinary sense of that word at all. The moment it begins to be dealt with as if it were one, the whole operation is off to a bad start.

The renewal of the liturgy ought to make a difference in catechisms and religion classes because it puts first things first. The Church's mission to "make disciples of all nations" is something it hopes to achieve from the altar outward. The "wondrous sacrament of the whole Church" is the visible and effective sign of God's love for men, revealed and given to us in Christ. If the Church comes to be known by Catholics generally in this way, rather than as a maiden aunt or a heavenly policeman, there is no end to the possibilities of disciplemaking.

As it is, the Church has put herself, through her schools, her catechism classes, and her textbooks, in the false position of seeming to be a schoolroom-style teacher, rather than a mother who forms her children in a spiritual home. Christianity has become something you "learn" (like irregular verbs or traffic regulations) rather than something you do, or are.

This is all wrong, of course. You meet God, you meet Jesus Christ on many occasions, but chiefly in that response to the Father's love which we call "worship." It is there that we come before Him as a people—there that He shows Himself to us best, both in the eucharistic food and in the "sacrament of the brother." Many things in this world tend to hide God, but the whole purpose of the sacraments is to disclose Him to us.

The liturgy at its best (as we hope it will be after it is reformed, in other words) is intended to be the chief teacher of men as to what God is like. He didn't choose books for the purpose, or schools, or charts, or blackboards. He chose a living human situation: men at prayer with His son, Jesus, in their midst. Our Lord can be known and known well in the action of the Mass if we don't wrap Him up in winding-sheets: sheets of incomprehensible language, of meaningless movement, of long-forgotten gesture, of unimportant word.

Catholics must be helped truly to meet Christ present in His Church. They must come to know Him as He knows the Father—with a personal knowing that means a growing love, a likeness, a share in His life and action. This knowledge is possible if the sacraments are celebrated well. Otherwise, all you can hope for is to tell Catholics what they must do and believe to "save their souls." You're left high and dry, busy drilling into them ways to avoid harmful influences that will destroy their faith and morals. Christianity can become a rule book, not a meeting with the God who saves.

This may sound as if we think no one can teach religion interestingly in a school-like situation. But, of course, that's not true. Some can and do. The point is, the school or CCD class or adult study club is the place to *prepare* to meet Christ sacramentally; it is not the place to meet Him in the full sign of word and bread. Catechisms (even good ones) can only talk about God; they are not a conversation with God. Worst of all, religion packaged in books and classes can give a totally wrong impression. Study aids of any kind must always point in two directions: *to the sacraments,* where the mystery of Christ is celebrated; *and to life,* where the mystery of Christ is lived.

You don't find the Council fathers confused on any of these points. They know, for example, that you must teach people who are outside the Church if they don't yet believe. Men can't come together to pray through the sacraments if they haven't any faith, or the right faith, in these signs. They must first believe and change their ways. (See *Constitution,* Article 9.) Even with believers, the Church "must prepare them for the sacraments, teach them to observe all that Christ has commanded, and invite them to all the works of charity, piety, and the apostolate."

The whole point seems to be that if we ever get serious about religion, Catholic-style, it will stop being a bore. We will meet Christ in all the places He waits to meet us—and He puts nobody to sleep!

12. The Difference in the Mass

What would it be like in this country if, by some magic, all of its parishes overnight were to celebrate Mass in the way proposed in the *Constitution on the Sacred Liturgy?*

It is impossible to know the answer to that question, but we can hazard a few guesses.

There would be a weekly experience of God's action in human lives, that much is sure.

People would come out of church on Sunday convinced that God had spoken to them—that Jesus Christ, whom they had just met, was in fact their priest and redeemer and friend.

They would know clearly the meaning of the action of praise in which the Savior had led them moments before.

Catholic worshipers would have seen, in a word, that the Mass was basically an action in two parts: a Bible service and a sacred meal, both of them calculated to excite faith and conclude in praise.

Simple rites would be easy to identify such as the entrance and the departure of the officers of the liturgy. Coming reverently into the area where the altar is located is simplicity itself; so is leaving. Getting altar breads and wine from some point *away from* the altar *to* the altar is likewise readily recognizable behavior. So is the washing of dishes—even though they be gold or silver dishes—after a meal.

The one hard thing to get across in a single, spoken prayer (or sung prayer, for it could just as easily be that) is the exact way Christians unite under Christ their Head to let God save them through an act of sacrifice that is happening now. It can't be Calvary repeated, in any sense. That notion is unthinkable, as Hebrews makes very clear (7, 27). It must be the mystery of the cross *done in sacrament*, not just its benefits made available *through* sacraments.

You see, don't you, how for the moment we're avoiding all

specific questions such as whether the people will be praying certain prayers in English and others in Latin on the magic "tomorrow morning" we're dreaming of? We don't especially care whether there are pews in the church, much less people kneeling in them at certain times, standing at others. We care only about the ultimate questions which the Council fathers care about.

For example, will there be anyone *at* the Mass fifty or one hundred years from now for whom to think up new rules? Will a Pakistani population tolerate a European way of praying forever? Will the desperately poor in the "inner city" or the "marginal populations" in rural areas ever come anywhere near a Catholic church, to be told they can't sing while they are going forward to receive the eucharist?

Those are the questions the *Constitution* is really concerned about if you read it carefully. There are some people spread around the Catholic world who are upset by the changes being made in the Mass, but in a very important sense, they don't matter. (Everyone matters tremendously, of course; we mean their concerns are ultimately not important ones.) God can save these worriers and bring them to heaven somehow.

The fact is that they have nothing vital to say on the question of how God's life can come to men by the billions who are alive on the earth at this writing. They have never thought of the problem. They prefer a Mass rite that is not much changed so that *they* will feel at home in it, never giving thought to the countless legions who will never feel anything in it, much less "at home," if it stays the way it is.

The Council fathers laid the axe to the root, as St. John the Baptist said once. They worked out certain clear principles for the commission on implementation of the *Constitution* to act on. These principles stipulate that the various rites should be marked by a "noble simplicity, . . . be short, clear, and unencumbered by useless repetitions . . . within the people's powers of comprehension, and . . . not require much explanation." (Article 34)

None of this is possible in a church the design of which works against the rites in their noble simplicity. The celebration of the mystery of Christ in its fullness can take place only in a building conceived and dedicated to this purpose.

That spells death to the long and complicated solemn Mass which wears everybody out and makes them wish they had risen earlier. The first move in this direction has come already. The "useless repetition" of the epistle and gospel in two languages has come to an end. So has the necessity of the priest's saying silently to himself what the choir or the congregation are supposed to say or sing (for example, the entrance song, the song at the preparation of the gifts, the song at communion time, and the meditative chant that comes after the first Scripture reading).

Another "useless repetition" which has disappeared is the celebrant's saying a second time, "Lord, I am not worthy," as he holds Christ's body aloft. He has just said it prior to his own communion, a few minutes before. The repeated "Lord, I am not worthy" by priest, then people, remains, but is fated to extinction.

If the people comprehend what is going on at Mass, both the words and the actions, they won't need much explanatory comment. It's great to hear the voice of an intelligent parishioner giving brief little cues (written freshly each Sunday) to help the congregation get ready for the canon, the communion rite, or whatever is coming up next. Still, these parts of the Mass action should speak for themselves and not need to be spoken about except on rare occasions.

The best example of all in this matter is the continuing need parishioners have of remembering what the canon is saying, all during its recitation by the priest. Oh, you can look down in your missal if you wish, but you really shouldn't have to. It's your leader's prayer which, by your strong "Amen" at the end, becomes your prayer. A pity you can't hear it, or, hearing it, can't understand it, isn't it? But that can be changed.

All the other sacraments besides the Mass are entirely in English now. That has been the case in this country since September 14, 1964. In the paragraph that permits this in principle (Article 36), the *Constitution* makes no distinction between "the Mass, the administration of the sacraments, or other parts of the liturgy." The framers say without qualification that the limits of the use of the mother tongue may be extended, since "this frequently may be of great advantage to the people." Any national grouping of bishops is free to make its proposals to the Holy See with respect to making comprehensible to the people the entire Mass rite.

Perhaps the best thing of all that the Council fathers said on these matters is that the "genius and talents of the various races and peoples" should be respected. (Article 37) "The Church has no wish to impose a rigid uniformity" (*ibid*.) in matters where the faith of Christian people or their general good does not require standardization. That doesn't mean that the men of Senegal and Micronesia are the only ones being thought of by the Council fathers. It means that the Swedish and the Spanish have different geniuses and talents, the English and the Irish, the people of Togo and the people of Malawi. Unity means life, in a world-wide Church. Uniformity, the bishops hint, can mean death.

If any reader deduces from the above reflections the simple formula, "Changes in the Mass, particularly language change, will solve all our problems," he will be quite wrong.

People must be prepared for change over a long, slow period. They cannot have things sprung on them all on a certain Sunday. They need to hear good, clear, biblical preaching week after week, year after year. They need sustained, skilled help for years on end to become a singing body of worshipers once more. They need first-class instruction apart from the Mass on exactly what Christ and we do together at the Mass.

Then and only then will "changes in the Mass" really change Christians.

13. Giving the Missal Back to the Priest

An interesting thing happened in the Catholic Church of the Roman rite some forty years ago. The people, who had been given nothing much to do at Mass, got hold of the priest's Mass-book and began to do everything about it.

We have spoken in previous chapters of the gradual capture of all the parts or "roles" by the priest. Over the course of centuries the liturgy, which had originally been a community drama, became a long "dramatic reading" by one man. Except for the people's receiving the eucharist, the priest, and his servers became the sole participants in the spoken and acted parts of the Mass.

The reasons for this were very logical. The priest was often the only man in town who could speak the language in which the play was written. Besides, as we've said before, the action got so complicated and so far away from the viewers that it was like producing *Hamlet* in a tunnel of stone and glass.

In the middle ages, the text of the Mass was preserved in a book for the priest's use called the "sacramentary." Oh, the people knew some ordinary chants and songs by heart (like the *Kyrie* and the *Credo*), but by and large a book was useless to them since the celebrant was saying all the prayers anyway. Besides, most of the people couldn't read, so owning a book wouldn't have mattered.

There was a second volume prescribed for use at Mass. It was called a "lectionary," that is, a selection of readings. The different epistles and gospels were in it for subdeacons and deacons to proclaim at the proper times. The Mass servers among our readers will recognize the lectionary from the "old days" as the book which is brought from the credence table during a solemn Mass. Still another kind of lectionary is the English book of epistles and gospels used in the pulpit or lectern. Parish lectors will recognize this book immediately.

After the Council of Trent, a "Roman Missal" was edited by scholars under the direction of Pope St. Pius v. There had been all sorts of variations in the way Mass was said—both in the different parts of Europe and in the various traditions in the monasteries and friaries. The new rule was that if the Mass had been said a certain way for at least two hundred years it could continue that way. Otherwise it was suppressed—brought to an end. This ruling explains the differences in the Carmelite or Dominican rite in the parishes to which some of you belong.

The last important detail to remember is that, just as in the case of Bibles, printers were not fully free to produce Mass-books in the people's languages. Vernacular Bibles began to be published fairly soon after the Council of Trent, but it wasn't until 1897 that vernacular missals were officially permitted to be printed for the people's use. There was a decree in 1857 which renewed the ancient prohibition: "It is not permitted to translate the Ordinary of the Mass. . . ," but in practice this prohibition was widely disregarded.

This may seem strange to us who are used to a great number of vernacular people's missals, but the Roman See seemed to think it had its reasons for not allowing vernacular missals during the two centuries after Trent. French politics had a lot to do with it. (A translation done by a certain M. Voisin was condemned in 1660.) So did the heresy of Jansenism and the continuing threat to the unity of the Church's faith comprised by the Reformers.

By the middle of the last century, however, these reasons had lost their force, and a widespread movement toward the production of vernacular missals for the people developed in Europe. Catholics were showing an increasing desire to pray the Mass in their own language. In fact, as early as 1822, Bishop Ambrose Maréchal of Boston successfully resisted an attempt by Rome to prohibit the first such English missal in the States by pointing out that "new translations" were forbidden. The one in question had long been in use in England and Ireland.

In the United States, in the 1920's, a representative of a publishing company in St. Paul, Minnesota, went to the Archbishop to ask his advice on publishing the *Saint Andrew's Daily Missal* in English. It had been produced by the Abbey of S. André in Bruges, Belgium (where Dom Gaspar Lefebvre, its editor, is still active, incidentally). The Archbishop said—like the man at the bar who tasted his first glass of water, straight —"It'll never go!" All things considered, he thought it couldn't succeed commercially.

In this matter, however, he was wrong. The publisher's instinct was right.

The *Saint Andrew's Daily Missal* was a pioneer. Other Mass-books followed—such as those edited by Father F. X. Lasance, a priest of the Columbus Diocese, and Fathers Callan and McHugh, two Dominicans who taught for years at the Maryknoll Seminary in Ossining, New York.

But the man who changed the face of the country, missal-wise, was a Brooklyn priest, Father Joseph Stedman, who was a chaplain to contemplative nuns. From their Monastery of the Precious Blood on Fort Hamilton Parkway he first produced a series of good-looking, low-cost novena booklets. Then Father Stedman "discovered" the Mass, and after that the Scriptures. During World War II his generally well-edited little Mass-book and New Testament went all around the world in khaki covers.

After World War II it got so that you could pick out the Protestants and the Catholics on Sunday mornings. They completed each other, so to say, by carrying off to church the two chief testimonies to God's living word in His Church: the Bible and the liturgy.

The only trouble was, the Catholics didn't really need all the prayers that were contained in their missals.

In reclaiming their own prayers from the priest, they took his too!

Just as the priest had for centuries been praying the people's prayers at Mass, so now the people were praying his. The priest's confession of sins with his servers, his preparation to read the gospel to the people, his prayers when he washed his hands, his exchange with his brothers in the sanctuary (*"Orate, fratres"*) and their answer (*"Suscipiat"*)—everybody began to read these prayers of his right along with him. If the people had lost their public lives in the liturgy, the priest now began to lose his private life.

Wait a minute! How is this chapter going to end? Have the Council fathers straightened *that* one out too?

Indeed they have. As soon as they said that everyone at the Mass, whether minister or layman, ". . . who has an office to perform, should do all of, but only, those parts which pertain to his office by the nature of the rite and the principles of liturgy" (Article 28), they took the priest's prayers away from the people. But if the bishops have taken the collect, the prayer over the gifts, the post-communion prayer, and the canon away from the layman, they have put the entrance and departure chants, the songs after Scripture readings, at the preparation of the gifts, and at communion back into his hands.

The people's Mass-book has a great future. It won't have nearly so much in it, but it will be twice as thick.

You've got the picture. Music!

The altar missal will have the priest's parts.

The lectionary will have the Scripture readings.

The people's Mass-book will have the people's parts: for example, the dialogued responses, the ordinary chants (Creed, Glory to God, and the like), and the proper chants such as those mentioned above, complete with musical settings.

What have the American bishops done about the question of distributing the roles correctly? They have decreed that the portions of the Mass recently put into English should be in altar missals only, not in hand missals. This means lectionaries in the pulpits, and cards or songbooks for the faithful. Several bishops have fostered genuinely active music commissions. These don't simply publish lists of approved and disapproved music. They are deep in the work of educating musically at a high standard.

"Look *up*," the Church is saying, "and lift up your hearts."

14. What a "People's Mass-Book" Should Look Like

"It is to be stressed that whenever rites, according to their specific nature, make provision for communal celebration involving the presence and active participation of the faithful, this way of celebrating them is to be preferred, so far as possible, to a celebration that is individual and quasi-private." So wrote the Catholic bishops of the world in their *Constitution on the Sacred Liturgy.* (Article 27)

Now, the Mass *is* such a celebration. Therefore, whenever possible, it should be dealt with as a public act rather than as a private prayer.

When a churchful of people at Mass spends half an hour in silence, this congregation has offended against the nature of the Mass. The servers may have "exercised a genuine liturgical function" (Article 29), but the celebrant, "readers, commentators, and members of the choir" (*ibid.*) have not.

It is fairly clear that, despite their "sincere piety and decorum," they are neither "deeply imbued with the spirit of the liturgy" nor "trained to perform their functions in a correct and orderly manner." (*Ibid.*) Why is that clear? Because if they were, each person would have exercised his proper role as he should have instead of failing to do certain important things. He may even have changed the whole nature of the rite by silence, inaction, or emphasis on the wrong matters during the course of the celebration.

The question is an important one. Ignorance may provide an excuse of some sort, but once it comes to be widely known that the Mass is true to its nature *only* if it both excites faith and manifests the faith of a believing people, we cannot plead ignorance any more. The Council fathers have dealt ignorance a deathblow by stressing over and over again the *total sign value* of every act of liturgy. Faith is both manifested and nourished to the degree that the signs of word and deed are understood, whether by those who make them, or by those for whom they are made.

How is the growth of faith through the liturgy to be ensured? Our document says: "To promote active participation, the people should be encouraged to take part by means of acclamations, responses, psalmody, antiphons, and songs, as well as by actions, gestures, and bodily attitudes. And at the proper times all should observe a reverent silence." (Article 30)

That's a pretty ambitious program. Before we get any deeper into the question, we ought to point out, not the value of reverent silence—for we Catholics have long known its value—but the new value which silence acquires by contrast with sound. Silence threatens to become a passive nothingness against a setting of more silence. Set carefully between blocs of verbal activity, song, and movement, it can become a positive, dynamic thing.

Now to our problem. Who is going to encourage all the parishioners in Western Christendom to musical activity of a high order? The challenge is tremendous, both as to quantity and quality of music. The place to start, it would seem, is the production of aids for such a program, aids of a kind that really help.

What sort of "aids" do we mean? We mean people's Mass-books more than anything else.

Not cards which have the English chants and responses, for already the whole Catholic populace has come to know these by heart and does not need the cards. (Within a few years, we might say in parenthesis, a single wording of the Mass formulary will probably unify the whole English-speaking world, giving us millions of people on all the continents who pray with this "sign of unity." English is, in fact, emerging as serviceable in a unique way among the family of languages—a role Latin once had in the West.) Another thing against cards is that if they feature hymns or parts of the Mass set to song, people quickly weary of repeating the same few melodies.

No, we have to have rich collections of good music that will be sufficiently varied to attract congregations strongly to the

idea of community song. Take the question of "acclamations."
After the Scriptures are proclaimed (whether the first reading,
the "epistle"—though that term is inaccurate if the Old Testament is read—or the second, the gospel), it is fitting to acclaim
joyously what our ears have just taken in.

For example, God has said that, with Him, "mercy tri-
umphs over judgment" (Jas. 2, 13; Feast of St. John Kanty,
October 20). We want to acknowledge somehow that our God
is the Lord, this great Lover who sent His Son to tell us that
henceforth we were to be judged "under the law of freedom."
(Jas. 2, 12) How shall we respond to this consoling truth we
have just heard? By turning to our Mass-book and there find-
ing either a musical phrase such as "Thanks be to God," or
those portions of Psalm 106 [107] and Proverbs 31 given as
the gradual verse and Alleluia on that feast, in a good setting
both as to melody and pitch.

In the same way, after we learn the generous service of the
master who, in Jesus' parable, "buckles his belt, seats them at
table, and waits on them" in the middle of the night (Lk. 12,
37; the same feast), we want to respond with "Sing your praise
to Christ, the Son of the living God," or something of the sort.
If the Scripture reading *really* moves us, in other words, our
thoughts need a tongue to express this fact.

Let's get specific about the whole matter.

A people's Mass-book needs to contain the following items
for use at a low Mass (besides the spoken responses to the
priest, which the people will come to know soon enough anyway):

(1) A large collection of processional (entrance) hymns,
and an equally large collection of recessional (exit) hymns
*in the spirit of the individual Sundays, feast days, and "com-
mons," such as that of martyrs.* Besides such hymns, there
should also be the proper introits in English, either the whole
psalm or other Scripture passage and its refrain (antiphon),
or a sizable portion of it. These can be set to the Gregorian
"psalm tones" for use at sung Masses; they do not need any
new approval in English because this music has so long been
approved. If new music is composed a local bishop must approve its use.

(2) Just as in the case of introits, so the verses provided at the beginning of the preparation of the gifts (formerly called the offertory rite) and during communion time need to be expanded. These verses are usually taken from the psalter too; in the same way, they can be substituted for by hymns *in their spirit*.

(3) The people's Mass-book *may* have the priest's prayers like the collects, the prefaces, and the canon, but these should appear in an appendix for home study. Otherwise the people will be reading them as before, whereas they should listen as this important material is read in their hearing (the "inner nature" of language).

(4) Lastly, there should be a variety of musical settings of the ordinary chants of priest and people: Glory to God; I Believe; Holy, Holy, Holy; and Lamb of God.

One last item that needs to be included, in a variety of forms, is the prayer of the faithful. This is a prayer for the needs of all the people which is now prescribed for after "The Lord be with you" following the homily or creed. The instruction of September 26, 1964, which implements the *Constitution* makes clear that this is required. Bishops can specify the forms this prayer may take, but it will ordinarily conclude with the collect "O God, our refuge and our strength" from the twenty-second Sunday after Pentecost, or another collect better suited to the occasion.

Finally, the people's Mass-book could contain a variety of sung Masses in whatever English-Latin formula prevails. New music should be written and approved constantly if our religion is to be a living thing.

But who will *write* all these fine chants and songs?

Great poets.

Great musicians.

Some of them, let's hope, are reading these lines right now.

15. A New Look at the Baptismal Rite

There is a remarkable short story, "The River," by Flannery O'Connor, the young woman writer from Georgia who died in 1964. It tells about a serious little boy named Harry whose young parents do some serious drinking. One day a "sitter" takes him to a revival meeting down by the river, where he hears about Jesus and baptism for the first time.

"What's that?" he asks.

"If I baptize you," the preacher says, "you'll be able to go to the kingdom of Christ. You'll be washed in the river of suffering, son, and you'll go by the deep river of life. Do you want that?"

Harry does. He won't ever have to go back to the apartment then, where his parents sometimes don't sleep off a large evening until one in the afternoon.

He comes home baptized, and his mother asks him what that ignorant preacher has been saying to him.

"He said I'm not the same now. I count."

The next day he goes back to the river and wades in, waist deep. This time he's going to baptize himself and keep on going until he finds the kingdom of Christ in the river. He starts under, gets a muddy mouthful, and spits it out, angry and sick. Someone has fooled him again! Then he loses his footing and gets pulled forward and down by a waiting current that grasps him like a hand. At that, after an initial surprise, "all his fury and fear left him . . . since he was moving quickly and knew he was getting somewhere."

A Christian is a person who didn't count before, but does now. He has been washed in "the River of Blood, the River of Pain" (those were the preacher's words). The passion of Christ is the event that gives power to the ordinary water in which you and I were baptized. "The baptism with which I must be baptized" was Jesus' description first of His bath in pain and then His being plunged into a waiting tomb.

We have been raised up from a drowning—in infancy, most of us—emerging as entirely new creatures in the kingdom of Christ. We die and live by way of a river: ". . . the stream of divine grace which flows from the paschal mystery of the passion, death, and resurrection of Christ, the fount from which all sacraments and sacramentals draw their power." (*Constitution*, Article 61)

Here again, the question the *Constitution* puts to us is whether a person could learn what is happening at a baptism just by going to one. Could this be just one more case like the eucharist (on which we've spent our last fourteen chapters) where, "With the passage of time . . . there have crept into the rites . . . certain features which have rendered their nature and purpose far from clear to the people of today?" (Article 62) In such case, some changes are necessary to adapt the baptismal rites to the needs of our times, just as changes are needed in the Mass.

The book which contains the rite of baptism is called a ritual. The Roman missal was first published in 1570; it fixed the rite of the Mass in the West from its first appearance. The Roman ritual, on the other hand, which came along in the early 1600's, had as its purpose supplying the rites to be used for the various sacraments if the rituals prepared by national hierarchies didn't get specific enough.

Gradually the process was reversed, so that now the Council fathers are saying that particular rituals should be prepared without delay by the proper authorities (the American and Canadian bishops, in our case) "in harmony with the new edition of the Roman ritual." (Article 63b) This "new edition" hasn't been produced yet. It will be the work of some years by scholars who are proceeding under the guidance of the commission for follow-up on the liturgy.

The American bishops published a collection of rites in English and Latin in 1954, and again in 1961. Then on April 2, 1964, they issued a decree which said that all the sacraments and sacramentals should be published in one book with the prayers in their entirety in both languages. That *Collectio Rituum,* as it is called, came out in September, 1964.

We should mention an important thing that happened on April 16, 1962, before the first session of Vatican II. It was related to the work of the Council, but on an interim basis and only indirectly. The Holy See published a rite for the baptism of adults in seven distinct stages or steps. This was immediately incorporated into the Roman ritual now in use. You wouldn't call this a revision of the rite so much as a rearrangement of its parts. It can be employed in any diocese where the bishop authorizes it, until the rite for the baptism of adults is revised.

If, for example, an unbaptized adult were to present himself for this sacrament, the first step would be a ceremony in which a name was given him, and he would be solemnly signed with the cross on all his senses. This indicates that Satan's hold is about to be broken and he is to be consecrated to God. In the *second step,* some weeks or months later, salt is placed on the candidate's tongue. This is a sign of the increasing enjoyment he should be deriving from the instruction he is receiving.

Steps three, four, and *five* are exorcisms or prayers bidding Satan to begone. God is to dwell in this temple now, namely the person who is to become a Christian. In the *sixth step* the Our Father and the Apostles' Creed are said by the catechumens before the whole Church (they had learned these prayers during step one). They are anointed with oil and have their ears and nostrils opened with the sign of spittle.

The *seventh step* prepares immediately for the sacrament. It is like a summing up of all that has gone before and is chiefly a repetition of stage one. In the middle of it comes the central baptismal rite itself, following which a white garment and a lighted candle are given the candidate as signs of his new life.

If you've been at a baby's baptism, you will immediately recognize the seven steps. They are all found there, and you may wonder what's so special about the rite for adults. The answer is nothing, really, except the apportionment of the stages over the period of instruction.

The Council fathers say that they want the catechumenate

restored in distinct steps (Article 64) and the baptismal rite for adults revised (Article 66), both in its simple and solemn forms. There is to be a new Mass composed "for the conferring of baptism." (Article 66) If there are any initiation rites of long standing among a particular people or in a particular country, elements of these are to be adapted to the Christian ritual wherever possible. (Article 65) Most important, at least as far as numbers go, is the Council's decision that babies shall be dealt with in a new rite for what they are: newborn babies! (Article 67) It's pretty shocking to parents to hear their lovely infants described in terms of a strong grip by Satan. Actually the exorcisms were composed for adults who were presumed to have "sown some wild oats."

If there are large numbers of babies—say fifteen or so in a suburban parish church on a Sunday—this fact is to be dealt with realistically in a revised rite. (Article 68) Also, there is to be a new short form of emergency baptism (Article 68) and a rite that is to be used later, different from the one in use now, of "supplying the ceremonies." The new rite will indicate that the little one is a Christian already.

Finally, baptized adults who are received into the Church also need a new rite. (Article 69) The present formula stands on a supposition which is almost never true, namely that the adult is a conscious, stubborn heretic who has knowingly held errors against the faith which he is finally ready to give up.

New, new, new! What was so wrong, for all those centuries, that the Church in Council felt it had to call for all these sweeping changes?

The central fact that cried out for change was that the signs of faith weren't speaking to Christians any more—weren't transmitting faith, weren't strengthening faith.

An adult catechumen, for example, should have had the beginnings of Christian faith stirred up in him through every gesture, every word, over a long period, and it wasn't happening. Parents of babies, godparents, and friends should have had their faith quickened by signs, and that wasn't happening either.

Therefore, the Church took steps—seven of them, at least, with more to come.

16. Confirmation, Anyone?

My grandfather's middle name was Nicholas. He became "James N. Sloyan" when he was about fifty years of age. He acquired the name from a church, St. Nicholas of Tolentine, when an Augustinian Father finally said to him before he was confirmed, "Well, you've got to take *something* for a middle name." They cared about the sacraments quite a bit in Knock, but my grandfather was on a fishing boat in the North Sea by the time the Bishop of Tuam managed to come for confirmation.

There are men in this world named William Gerard Griffin and William Gerard Pike because neither of them really wanted a second name. They did want the fullness of the Holy Spirit, however, and on that occasion took their revenge on their instructor by taking his name as their own.

Why all the fuss about names on the occasion of receiving the sacrament of confirmation? The whole thing is custom, really. Church law doesn't get too specific about it. There is no mention of a name at confirmation in the Code of Canon Law, for example, although there is a suggestion from the Second Plenary Council of Baltimore (1866) that names be written out on a card from which pastors are to read while the bishop is confirming. Pastors should see to it that parents choose a saint's name for babies at baptism, says our Western Church law, but if they can't be made to do so, a patron saint should be entered in the baptismal register. The custom of a *new* name has a much longer history than that of a saint's name, since baptism is in fact the gateway to new life. Very early in the Church, Christians were taking the names of apostles and martyrs or making up names like "Gift of God" or "Born Again."

We are dwelling on this question because a "confirmation name" is basically unconnected with the reality of the Spirit in confirmation. Yet, these matters—like the spittle placed on a baby's nostrils—are blown up out of all proportion in the popular mind.

A friend of mine once took it on herself to ask a few dozen adult Catholics, in the space of two days, their clearest recollection of confirmation. Do you know what it was? Worry over how hard the bishop would strike them on the cheek! That is what you call canonizing the nonessential. Yet we have done something quite like that with the various rites in the sacraments themselves over the course of centuries.

There is only one article on confirmation in the *Constitution on the Sacred Liturgy* (Article 71), but it is a fairly long one, and it is in two paragraphs. As you might expect, the proposal is made that Christians should be confirmed within the Mass "when convenient. . . ." Because the bishop is the one who usually confirms in the Roman rite, it will fall to him to decide whether it is convenient or not. The reason underlying this, like that for a special new Mass "for the conferring of baptism," is not the shallow principle: "Mass with everything." No, the reason is historical and, at the bottom, doctrinal. It is rooted in the very nature and purpose of the sacrament of confirmation.

The Council fathers say:

"The rite of confirmation is to be revised and the intimate connection which this sacrament has with the whole of Christian initiation is to be more clearly set forth; for this reason it is fitting for candidates to renew their baptismal promises just before they are confirmed." (Article 71)

In the first centuries of the Church's life, there was no clear-cut distinction made between baptism and confirmation, so closely were these two rites joined. There was really only a single rite of initiation into life in Christ, and this was performed in three stages: the plunging into water (or pouring of water on one who was half-immersed) for the remission of sins, followed by an anointing which made one Christ-like; the placing of the bishop's hands on the newly baptized, sometimes accompanied by a second anointing which "sealed" him; then the eucharist, the joyful family meal of all who receive their strength from the living bread that has come down from heaven.

All the early writings that remain to us make it clear that when adults (and later babies) were initiated into Christian life, the three signs were always present. It is by no means easy to isolate confirmation in the series in the first three centuries. Yet an invoking of the Spirit, sometimes called a "sealing"—that is, a stamping, as of hot wax with a signet ring, or a sealing off, as of perfume in a jar—keeps persisting in the early writings.

These different figurative ways of speaking about stage two in the threefold rite always seem to be describing a special gift of the Holy Spirit, an extra. He has been given first at baptism. After this bath of rebirth, the Church calls on Him again, as it were, to give to those newly reborn a "portion of the kingdom of heaven according to the holy and certain promise of our Lord Jesus Christ." (That prayer is from the late second-century and was said when the balm to be used in anointing the baptized on whom hands were laid was blessed.) First, the Holy Spirit was spoken of as having begotten God's servants by water. Then follows a prayer which begins: "Send on them now the Holy Spirit, the Consoler. . . ."

Gradually, this "sealing" came to be regarded as a completion or perfection of baptism. A work begun in baptism by the Father and the Son, some Church Fathers wrote, was perfected when the Holy Spirit came. In Christ we die and are reborn, and the Holy Spirit is the "spiritual seal" of this (so said St. Ambrose). He sees to it that we are able to retain the brightness of Christ's image and grace. The Holy Spirit, in other words, makes an initial work of God complete. Like the sweet odor of chrism, the Christian perfected or sealed by the Spirit spreads the fragrance of Christ by the holiness of his life.

Confirmation, therefore, means *perfection* or *addition* more basically than strengthening, though the latter idea is not absent. That notion came later—along with the whole imagery of soldiers, battle, and the like. The basic significance of confirmation in the New Testament and the early Fathers is that with it comes the gift of the Spirit in His fullness. He comes to us as a pledge or "down payment"—a sign of more yet to come as we grow in grace.

Meanwhile, when He is with us in the relative fullness of the present time, Christian life is basically a life of the Spirit. It is at the same time quite correct to say that confirmation prepares us for our first communion, because the latter sacred sign always came third in the initiation series. Eucharistic life befits perfected, that is confirmed, Christians.

It is no wonder that Christians should be confirmed within the Mass "when convenient" and should renew their baptismal promises just before they are confirmed. The three stages of initiation into Christ should not be totally separated, even though many are baptized in infancy, receive their first eucharist at seven, and are confirmed at twelve—or fifty. The Council fathers are equivalently saying that if the right order in the three stages of Christian initiation cannot be kept, something should be done to remind us what the right order is.

This should help us remember what confirmation is, this "fixing in" of baptism which prepares us for the eucharist, and what it does.

It seems safe to assume that most adult Catholics have been confirmed. If they are Eastern rite Catholics or Western rite Catholics from Spanish-speaking backgrounds, they were doubtless confirmed as babies. Some were confirmed immediately before their first communion, as the Code of Canon Law specifies. But most, by long-standing custom, received this sacrament at the beginning of adolescence—in the upper years of elementary school.

They may have worried about the bishop's tap on the cheek. (Actually, it's a holdover from his kiss of peace which was an embrace with grown-ups but a mere touch with babies!) Neither this tap, nor the questions he might ask in catechizing them, were paramount. What is important is that this rite should be what it is meant to be in the lives of Christians: a sign whereby they know the Spirit has come to them in His fullness.

That means that a Christian needs to renew the spirit of his confirmation at certain solemn times after receiving it in childhood. A serious retreat is a time like that. So is engagement, or the marriage in which it ends. Religious profession and the first steps toward the priesthood are still other times to recapture the spirit of one's confirmation.

This sacrament is received only once, and its effects last forever. We all need to ask ourselves periodically, "Have its effects touched my life?"

17. Making a Virtue Out of Penance

Part of Martin Luther's complaint against his fellow Catholics when he was the prior of the Augustinian house at Wittenberg and biblical lecturer in its tiny university was that they wanted to avoid doing penance. The whole scheme for raising money to complete St. Peter's Basilica in Rome was pretty questionable, but then the Italians had been "milking" the Germans for years. What disturbed the young scholar-preacher was not the longstanding Roman technique of gouging under the guise of piety. It was that his fellow German Catholics had such a bad outlook on doing penance that they would go to any lengths to escape the punishments of purgatory, even separating themselves from large sums of cash.

That, of course, was what the whole sixteenth-century struggle on indulgences was about, at least at the start: either escaping purgatory or lessening its likelihood for oneself or one's dear ones through alms. Dr. Luther at first didn't object to schemes that seemed to promise a lighter sentence through giving gifts of money. His initial objection was to wanting to go scot-free, that is, not satisfy for one's sins through suffering at all. *Poena* means punishment, he said. It is the very essence of *poenitentia* to accept the punishment you deserve for your offenses against God's love.

Jesus had said that unless men did penance they would all perish. Running away from purification through pain, both in life and in death, was the basic sickness of the German Church according to the mind of the young Luther.

Later he learned (from reading the New Testament in Greek in the edition of Erasmus) that the original gospel word for penance isn't rooted in the word for penalty, but basically means a change of heart. That is what it meant for Jesus, who of course did not speak in Greek. "Do penance" was equiva-

lent in Aramaic to "Turn around in your tracks." If you've
been traveling north go south, if east turn west.

Actually, this didn't affect Luther's thinking much. What he
wanted was a change of mind and heart, the beginnings of
faith in other words, the acceptance of all that God was saying to man, in a spirit of perfect trust.

There is no difference between Luther and Catholic teaching on this point, though there was (and sadly is) a gap between the reminder of Catholic teaching provided by Luther,
and Catholic practice. Unless we do penance we shall never
see the kingdom. The punishment of purgatory may be a part
of the penance for us. God alone knows. But that we must
turn around in our tracks, "be converted," and in general feel
the pain of the difference between what we are and what we
are called to be, there can be no doubt.

The title of this chapter speaks of "making a virtue out of
penance." It is one already, of course. The only trouble is,
do we know this or do we just "go to confession"? A virtue is
a continuous state of commitment to God who is good. All
men are sinners before God who hates sin. To be continually
conscious of this fact—with the appropriate resolve to repent
of one's sins and amend one's life—is to be virtuous. On occasion the virtue of penance will find expression in the great
act of penance, namely confessing one's sinfulness before the
whole Church. This sacrament is not the only act of penance,
of course, but it stands out among all the rest.

Every Catholic has probably heard of public penitential
practices in the early centuries. People guilty of sins like deny-
ing Christ and worshiping idols (to save their skins) or murder or adultery had to abstain from receiving the eucharist for
their remaining adult lifetimes, and do public penance besides.
They dressed in rough clothing, disfigured their faces with
ashes, and in general did hard things to make amends for their
folly in turning against Christ and His love.

Later, arrangements were worked out which made it easier
to be received back into the communion of the Church. For
one thing, you could be forgiven by the bishop long before
you reached old age and live a regular eucharistic life again.
Another important detail was that ordinary priests were al-

lowed to reconcile sinners to the Church, not bishops only. Finally, the whole matter came to have a private character rather than a public one. This saved people considerable humiliation and shame, but it also made them forget that sin is not only an offense against God but also against the Church.

Most of us would prefer to tell our sins to a priest quietly in the dark to having them made public in a solemn church service, if that is the choice offered. An important question is, though, have we committed the kinds of sins that are already public knowledge (like blasphemy, open adultery, apostasy from faith), or are our sins the secret, mean little ones that most people commit? When the Church changed the rules on the kinds of sins confessed and forgiven, it almost necessarily altered the way in which they would be forgiven. "Public sins, public penance; private sins, private penance" is a formula that seems to make a lot of sense.

Nonetheless, every sin, even the meanest little private thoughts of envy, are an offense against one's brother, against the Church, against all men. In a way, sin has no "private character." It is always public, always an attack on the *plebs sancta* or holy people of God.

The *Constitution* says that "The rite and formulas for the sacrament of penance are to be revised so that they more clearly express both the nature and effect of the sacrament." (Article 72)

It becomes easier to see how and why this sacrament needs revision now that we are receiving it in English. The priest greets us with a prayer which asks that we may confess well. Then, after we have done so, and he has spoken to us if he wishes to, he says the two prayers begging mercy, indulgence, and forgiveness of our sins which always come after the Confiteor. This is a tip-off. The basic framework of this sacrament is that prayer. Many of our parents and grandparents have the first half of the Confiteor as their form of confession. They break off at "through my most grievous fault" to tell their sins.

After his two short, Confiteor-concluding prayers the priest asks the Lord Jesus Christ to forgive us, and says that he himself forgives us. There is a leftover phrase from centuries that speaks of absolving us "from excommunication, interdict, and censure insofar as I am able and you have need." Actually, the whole scheme for removing all three such penalties is quite different now in Church law. The priest in the confessional can occasionally remit them, but he always does so after consulting his bishop (the penitent remains anonymous, of course) and never simply by that casual phrase. Therefore seminary professors often tell future confessors to omit it. It sounds pretty silly with eight-year-olds—and with sixty-eight-year-olds too, when you know the words don't accomplish what they say.

The rite of penance needs revision because it is so legal-sounding as it now stands. It gives the impression that the priest is a judge on the bench who can only say "Not guilty." The secrecy is fine but the black-box-in-the-corner mentality isn't so fine. Actually, the whole Church has reason to rejoice when sinners, great and small, either make their peace with Christ or have the guilt of lesser sins removed. There ought to be some way to express this.

The best thing we can do now is avoid making an act of contrition while the priest is speaking to us. Merest courtesy on both sides requires this. But it's also good to know—once you hear the absolution formula clearly—that theologians of the liturgy are hard at work to improve it. A good start is being made in some dioceses with "celebrations of penance." This is a devotion made up of hymns and Bible-readings which feature God's fatherly love and forgiveness. In the midst of them there is set either the sacrament of penance itself or else a blessing, a sacramental which removes the guilt of venial sins and imperfections. This is a most impressive ceremonial. It helps those who take part realize how all human guilt does harm to all of us and is not directed to God alone.

We can be sure that in any revision of the rite of penance several things will be changed: the physical setting of the sacrament, perhaps gestures such as the priest's putting his stole on the head of the one forgiven, and most of all the Scripture readings and prayers used.

Will it take longer? Probably. Does this mean that people will confess less frequently? In a sense they couldn't be confessing less frequently than now. After the revision, it is hoped more people who need this sacrament will be receiving it, and on much better terms. Those who do not need it would be receiving remission of their lesser guilt through a sacramental of repentance—a much more fitting means.

18. The Christian Way of Death

Not long ago the writer participated in the funeral Mass of a great Christian. She was a loving wife and faithful mother of a family which knows quite a lot about liturgical prayer. Wonderful, true things were said about her by a preacher who knew her well. He said truer things about her, in some respects, than the funeral liturgy itself said, for the gloom which the funeral liturgy has acquired during the past centuries is really far removed from what the Church teaches about Christian death.

This spirit of gloom comes through clearly at the blessing of the Christian's body after Mass, for example, just before it is taken to be laid in the earth. "O Lord, do not bring your servant to trial . . . We implore you . . . do not let the verdict of your judgment go against him . . . Rather . . . may he escape the sentence which he deserves. . . ." And again: "I am in fear and trembling at the judgment and the wrath that is to come . . . As you come to judge the world by fire."

In a moment we can speak about how the liturgy got to be that way. But first we need to point out how strongly the bishops at the Second Vatican Council have stated their desire that the liturgy should express the joys of the departed Christian's victory in the risen Christ. Their thoughts on Christian death are expressed briefly, but are very much to the point:

"The rite for the burial of the dead should express more clearly the paschal character of Christian death, and should correspond more closely to the circumstances and traditions found in various regions. This holds good also for the liturgical color to be used." (Article 81)

Question: What is the "paschal character of Christian death?"

Answer: It is simply that the departed Christian shares in Christ's death and rises up to a new life with Him.

Question: Does the present rite of burial have a paschal character?

Answer: It has a half paschal character, or three quarters. Not a whole one.

Question: Explain that a little.

Answer: Gladly. You see, the text of the Mass offered on the occasion of a burial and the prayers that follow it are very clear on the point that death is a penalty for sin. They also show that Jesus will be our judge on the last day, separating "sheep from goats," as He himself said. Finally, there is no confusion in the liturgy of death on the point that it is only by God's mercy that any of us sinners are saved, and will be raised up on the last day.

Questioner (beginning to be interested): Well, that sounds like good Christian doctrine to me. How "paschal" can you get?

Answer: Considerably more. For example, St. Paul says: "For we were buried with him [Jesus Christ] by means of baptism into death . . . if we have been united with him in the likeness of his death, we shall be so in the likeness of his resurrection also." (Rom. 6, 4–5) In another place he writes: ". . . Christ died for all, in order that they who are alive may live no longer for themselves, but for him who died for them and rose again . . . If then any man is in Christ, he is a new creature; the former things have passed away; behold, they are made new!" (2 Cor. 5, 15–17)

What those marvelous passages are saying is that the baptized Christian has already had his feet set on the path of new life. He has lived his lifetime as part of a "new world." Throughout his days, he has been drinking the cup of salvation and eating the bread of eternal life. Could you learn any of this at his funeral Mass—even presuming that all its prayers and readings were in English? Not very readily.

On the contrary, in the present rite he is almost presumed to be a serious sinner. If he has had a sacramental life that will raise him up from the dead, you cannot learn this from the liturgy. That he will rise again by God's mercy, somehow, is all the burial rite seems to know.

Let's look at the epistle of the Funeral Mass. That has a

paschal character—almost. St. Paul is making it clear to the Christians in Thessalonica that, when our Lord comes back at the end of the world, they won't be any worse off for having died than those who are still alive. But this, in itself, says little about the new and glorious life of the faithful departed.

In the gospel, our Lord is telling Martha that, while the dead will rise up from their graves (which she already believes, being a pious Jew of the Pharisee party), it is He who will make the difference. To believe that He is the Messiah is to have the faith that ensures a person that he shall never die. That is "paschal faith," all right—though without any explicit reference to the sacraments which for a lifetime were the signs of that faith.

Then, in the entrance song and communion song, there is a good sentiment from a Jewish book of piety known as the fourth book of Ezra. It asks God for light and peace and rest for the dead because He is merciful.

Lastly, the preface of the Mass says that life is changed for the dead, not taken away.

Having reported on these better parts of the requiem Mass, we must point out that the rest is all about escaping the pains of hell. The "sequence" or song after the epistle is entitled "Day of Wrath," and is far from expressing a paschal joy. The song at the preparation of the gifts is an Old Testament prayer. In it, the Lord Jesus as king of glory is implored to deliver the souls of the departed faithful from the pains of hell. The fact that *sheol* or the nether-world of Hebrew belief is meant, rather than the state of damnation, provides the Christian family with very little comfort. "Hell" means eternal loss to the Catholic.

As we've mentioned at the beginning, the prayer of absolution over the body begs mercy on this Christian that he may "escape the judgment of condemnation" and "the wrath to come, sore distress and wretchedness on that great and bitter day" of final judgment.

Do we Christians believe all this, discounting some of the vivid imagery of late Jewish poetry? Indeed we do! There *will* be a judgment. We *are* all sinners. We hope to escape the full consequences of our sins by God's mercy.

But is this the best possible way to pray, as a Church, about the meaning of Christian death? Indeed it is not. It can be much improved. The Council fathers demand this improvement.

You see, the Church in its early centuries had a wonderful understanding of the Old Testament and of the way in which everything in it was fulfilled in Christ. The poets who composed our first liturgy of death could write about escape from "the lion's mouth" and "the deep pit" and be thinking, all the while, about the waters of baptism and the bread and wine of the eucharist. These, they knew, were God's answer to the terrors of death.

In the middle ages, however, a generation came along that knew all about those terrors (which they interpreted literally, knowing nothing of Hebrew poetry) and a whole set of fresh ones (fires that destroyed entire towns, the "black death," petty tyrants at whose hands the poor could expect no justice whatever in this life). The medieval poets of the liturgy, who meditated on the Old Testament imagery, didn't know how to highlight the biblical hope and poured on even more gloom.

The result? Well, as we've said, if there happens to be a Christian who has lived a lifetime faithful to God's gifts and who has "worked toward death" all his life, you can't learn that fact by going to his funeral. It is as though there were no such Christians. The reality is, of course, that this is the only kind of Christian there is supposed to be.

It should be helpful to add that the *Constitution* is just as interested in straightening out the rite of anointing the sick (see Articles 73 and 75) and the sacrament of the eucharist for the dying, *viaticum* (see Article 74), as it is in setting the liturgy of the dead straight. Your anointings should heal you and instruct you while you're still fully conscious and able to profit by them. After all, they work in the ordinary way of signs.

Even though you may not see the white vestments at your funeral, or may not hear the *Alleluias* ring out, or the mourners consoled with the great Scripture readings about the paschal mystery in its fullness, that's the way it ought to be, and hopefully that is the way it will be by the time you come to die.

19. Priestly Ordination and the Bishop's Book

A priest is ordained to bring God's word to men. He does this through preaching the gospel and breaking bread, the effective signs of the presence among us of God's Word made flesh.

A priest is given spiritual power over the sacramental body of Christ in the rite of the eucharist. He is given power over His mystical body the Church in a variety of ways. The sacrament of penance is perhaps the chief of these ways.

A priest is, by definition, a teacher of heavenly wisdom, a father of the poor, a comforter of the afflicted. He should be a deeply learned man but his is not a "learned profession" in the sense that it is not defined by the pursuit of knowledge. If a priest is an educator in school, an organizer of projects, a marshaler of human energies, he is any of these things only insofar as they serve his major commitment: to engage in a ministry that sanctifies the people of God.

This is just a roundabout way of saying that a priest exists for priestly work, and priestly work is leading people in sacramental prayer. All of a man's priestly duties, whether at the altar or away from it, are so many means of grace to him, just as all of a layman's activities, whether at Mass or on the job, are so many means of grace to him.

We need to keep in mind that a priest's priesthood is a derived thing. This is so not just in the sense that all power in the Church is a share in the power of Christ. Something more is meant, namely that while a priest has an independent existence and a job to do (like anyone in the Church), he has them in relation to a bishop. All priests are related sacramentally, that is as priests, to the bishops they assist.

This is equally true of secular priests and regulars (men who live by a religious rule). The latter are related, in their status as "religious," to their religious superiors. They are related in the exercise of their priesthood to their bishops. And a bishop's whole meaning in the Church is that he leads men in the prayer of Christ.

This is an important matter.

It is important because the Church is always in danger of forgetting what the essence of priesthood is. You see advertisements in Catholic magazines that try to interest young men in this calling by saying that they can be school teachers or scientists or youth leaders as well as priests. That's like giving advice on how to be happy though married. You ought to be happy because you're married—through your marriage, in other words. You ought to be humanly satisfied in the state of priesthood and not through things extraneous to it.

Teaching and working in a laboratory and building character through sports are things that anyone can do. Even priests can do them—though at times their doing them is a terrible waste of manpower.

A priest can do a few important things that no one else can do. He can preach salvation to men in the setting of those healing, saving signs which we call sacraments, and he can lead in offering the sacrificial meal. This is his role, his task in the Church. It is a role so badly needed that one should be filled with sorrow at seeing a priest turned to other tasks or kept from doing what he alone—in relation to a bishop—can do.

All these matters are better dealt with by the *Constitution on the Sacred Liturgy* as a whole, you might say, than by any particular paragraphs in it. As a matter of fact, it is Article 76 which deals explicitly with the way men receive holy orders. There are also three important articles (15, 16, and 17) on how seminary studies on the liturgy and all the branches of theology must be improved, and how changes must be made in the prayer lives of seminarians.

Still, the *Constitution* should have a great impact on the priesthood of the future by defining, practically speaking, in every one of its one hundred and thirty articles, what a priest is in relation to the whole Christian community. It does this by discussing the chief work of a priest: worship.

By this time, the reader will be thinking to himself: "There

is one article in the *Constitution* that discusses the ordination
sacrament? Very well. It's got to say, 'Work the whole thing
over.' Right?"

Right.

And here it is:

"Both the ceremonies and texts of the ordination rites are
to be revised. The address given by the bishop at the beginning of each ordination or consecration may be in the mother
tongue.

"When a bishop is consecrated, the laying on of hands may
be done by all the bishops present." (Article 76)

The book in which these ordination and consecration rites
are contained is called the Pontifical. We have called it "The
Bishop's Book" in the title of this chapter, for that's what it is.
The name is derived from a Latin word for bishop, *"pontifex."*
All the other liturgical books are also to be revised (remember Article 25), namely the missal, ritual, and the book of the
divine office. "The revision of the liturgical books must carefully attend to the provision of rubrics for the people's parts
as well." (Article 31)

When all this has come to pass, attending a priest's ordination should be the best possible incentive to a young man for
considering this role of service for himself.

The way things are now, ordination ceremonies are impressive for a variety of reasons: (a) because by them the actual
transmission of priestly power takes place, and Catholic people have faith in this mystery; (b) because Don or Mike is
becoming a priest during the ceremonies, and this means an
awful lot to the Clavelli family or to the Friends of Don Peter-
son, Incorporated; (c) because all the new priests can be seen
and heard concelebrating Mass aloud in strong voices; (d) because the rite is long and tedious and, therefore, must signify
a great deal.

Actually, however, none of these reasons is sufficient to
satisfy the sacramental principle. Recall what the principle is.
The prayers and rites must be signs so expressive of the inner
reality that the person who already believes in Christian
priesthood has a great experience and understanding of its
being passed along. This is true, up to a certain point, of *all*

who are present at the celebration of a sacrament, but the persons really concerned are the recipients of the sacrament. They can follow the inquiries and the exhortations well enough; besides, they've studied all about the rite beforehand.

Still, in its present unreformed condition, the "sign" of holy orders is as muted and muffled as any we have in the Church, even to the new priests. It also proves quite shocking in English to parents and friends when the bishop determines aloud that the young men are not illegitimate (in fact or at law), nor marked by a dissolute life.

We bring boys and young men on trips to seminaries to show them what priestly preparation is like. They should be invited to an ordination as the best way to unfold the mystery of priestly life to them. At the moment, that perfectly reasonable technique doesn't work very well. Whether one has a book or no book in hand, the ordination rite is not a very meaningful sign unless one has an intensely personal interest in it.

The special reason why "The Bishop's Book" needs revision is that its ceremonies were composed during a period when bishops' actions were being patterned on those of kings. Instead of taking part in his pontifical rites as a father, the bishop sat on his throne like a noble lord. The bishop is a shepherd, but it is difficult to recognize him as one so long as so few shepherds are discovered holding court.

As of now a bishop's consecration resembles nothing so much as the pomp of Byzantine court ritual. But the day is coming when the poorest of the poor can be invited to come in droves to see a bishop consecrated or priests ordained, so that they will get the best glimpse they ever had of the priestly love and power of Christ!

20. How to Act if You Have a Vocation – to Marriage

Once upon a time there was a young man studying for the priesthood who dropped out of the seminary shortly before the time came for his ordination. He made this move after much prayer and thought and considerable wise counsel. His father was not so wise. He wept.

"Jim," he said, "you have no idea what this meant to me. I mean, the idea of having a son a priest."

"Dad," said the young man, "that's exactly the way I got to thinking."

Parents don't necessarily know what is best for their children in the question of vocation. Every son and daughter is entitled to the same freedom of choice that his parents had in choosing their own vocation.

This is not a vote for the folly of youth against the wisdom of age. It is a vote for persons: older persons, younger persons, middle-aged children. Many of them (say 100 per cent or thereabouts) have divine vocations. Each vocation is distinct. None is transferable. Individuals are called to holiness in Christ in virtue of their baptism, which confirmation seals. This is the real Christian vocation, and it forms the foundation of everything else that a Christian may do. Besides, because he is a person he must ultimately decide for himself how he means to work out his salvation.

There are a few different possibilities, as everyone knows. Priesthood is one kind of service to the whole Church. A "common life" of prayer and good works is another. These are minority callings, numerically speaking: important enough in their way, terribly important, but not in the main current, so to say. The great majority of mankind is called by God to marry.

When Christians marry theirs is a holy state for the simple reason that they are persons in the Church. In that sense, however, unmarried Christians are just as much in a holy state. The special holiness of marriage must lie elsewhere.

Is it that children come of marriage, and that it is, therefore, the "source" of the Church? It is probably correct enough to say that, but one might add that marriage is sacred for the prior reason that *human beings* are born of it! Jewish marriage is sacred because holy offspring are born of it, and so it is with all those who marry and try to serve God.

This really leaves us asking whether Christian marriage is holy because marriage generally is holy, and whether this is but a special case of it.

St. Paul helped us solve the difficulty. He said that when a man and woman become a single body, as Scripture says (see Gen. 2, 24), there is a great truth hidden here, a mystery, a secret like the secret design God has had from eternity to bring us to Himself. For his part, Paul wished to refer the sign of marriage to Christ and His Church. (See Eph. 5, 32.)

The Apostle helped set us on the path of seeing in each Christian marriage a visible image of the close relation between Jesus, the husband, and His beloved wife, the whole company of believers in Him. Every time two who are baptized marry there is one more reminder to the world of how much Christ loves His bride. Reading the sign the other way around (St. Paul did this, too), we see that the love our Savior has for the Church, all glorious, "not having spot or wrinkle or any such thing," is the great pattern for a man who sets about loving his wife for a lifetime. He loves her as he does himself, for she is himself. (See Eph. 5, 28–30.)

Examining all those passages from Scripture—and our Lord quoted the one from Genesis to very much the same effect —you can see why it is that, even though most men marry, a Christian's call to marriage stands for something much holier than marriage itself. It is a lifelong symbol of the whole drama of salvation. Every newlywed couple represents, in miniature, the full sweep of salvation's story for all mankind.

What is God like? How much does He love us? *How* does He love us? Look to the nearest prayerful married couple to find out. They are the great sign. In their love and union we know something of the depths of the mystery of our life in God, our life in Christ.

If a married couple is a sign of God's secret design, the question can be fairly asked, "Isn't matrimony one of the clearest in the whole family of symbols which we call sacraments?" Undoubtedly it is. You can, at least, see two persons standing close to each other, hands clasped, and hear them say they take each other as man and wife "until death do us part." There is the visible, audible declaration of intent to be faithful to each other for a lifetime. What more could we ask by way of a sign that speaks clearly?

Well, said the Council fathers, we should put this sacrament within the Mass whenever possible. It ought to come after the homily has been preached and before the prayer of the faithful has been said. Moreover, the long prayer that calls on God's help for the bride ("May she be the beloved of her husband, as was Rachel; wise, as was Rebecca; long-lived and loyal, as was Sara") should be amended so that it includes the poor bridegroom! (See *Constitution*, Article 78.) Needless to say, it should be read in the people's language.

The same article says in the second paragraph that, if ever the sacrament of marriage is celebrated apart from Mass, "the epistle and gospel from the nuptial Mass are to be read at the beginning of the rite." (You will find them in your New Testament: Ephesians 5, 22–23, and Matthew 19, 3–6.) Moreover, the nuptial blessing should always be given to the couple. Up until now, it was given only to two Catholics on the occasion of the first marriage of each.

We haven't yet mentioned what we've come to expect in discussions of the *Constitution,* namely the demand for the revision and enrichment of the marriage rite. It's there, though. Article 77 is the place. In the new rite which the conciliar commission on follow-up in the liturgy has been told to draw up, the grace of the sacrament must be more clearly signified. More than that, the duties of the two who are marrying must be taught them within the rite.

Doesn't that happen already? Again, yes and no. Actually, the rite given in the Roman ritual for celebrating marriage is very brief. It starts off with the question, "Owen Bowen, do you take Ann Mahon, here present . . . ?" and so on. In other words, the priest, who is one of the official witnesses, gets to the business of the sacramental consent right away.

Those of you who have been to Catholic weddings will recall a formula of exhortation that often comes first. It needn't come however. A homily, or even some extemporaneous remarks, can replace it. Most priests read this formula, though. It begins: "Dear friends in Christ: as you know, you are about to enter into a union that is most sacred and serious, . . ." This reminder was written by a San Francisco priest, years ago.

Recently, more was added to this exhortation in another spirit. It was put in brackets, and in that twofold form it appears in the *Collectio Rituum* approved by the National Conference of Bishops of the United States of America (1964). Any national group of bishops is free to compose its own formula of exhortation and place it directly within the rite. Very probably our bishops did not depart from long-standing United States practice because they were awaiting the new Roman rite of marriage—a wise enough procedure.

When the new rite is produced, though, this won't mean the end of initiative on the part of the different countries. The "competent territorial ecclesiastical authority . . . is free to draw up its own rite suited to the usages of place and people." (Article 77) In this connection, a four-hundred-year-old phrase from the Council of Trent is quoted which reminds Catholics that various regions may, by all means, retain praiseworthy customs and ceremonies connected with marriage. If this is done, the entire spirit of French Canada or Croatian Yugoslavia or Togo or Chad can be reflected in the marriage rite.

Every time we read one of these articles from the Council document, we see again how essential it is that the great Christian poets and scholars of a nation be put at this task by their bishops. Who, after all, knows the spirit of a Christian people if not their bards, their folklorists, their sociologists, their theologians?

How much may we not look forward to experiencing the formative power of the liturgy if all the countries of the world stay faithful to the requirements of the *Constitution!*

21. Sacramentals Change if the Rites of Sacraments Do

If one were asked to summarize the teaching of Vatican II on the liturgy, he would have to say that the Council fathers were chiefly interested that "the faithful should easily understand the sacramental signs." (Article 59)

"The sacraments are the signs of the present-working-out of the salvation of men," someone has written. That is quite true. Christ himself is present in His word, for it is He who speaks whenever the Scriptures are proclaimed in church. It is also He who acts, or rather it is the Father who acts through Him, every time a congregation led by its ministering priest uses water or oil, bread and wine, salt, spittle, or solemn speech.

The essential requirement is that priests and people should see Christ at work in the very act of saving them *in the signs they celebrate*. In the nature of the case, signs cannot give true worship to God, build up the body of Christ, or impart grace to men unless they instruct, that is, tell men what is happening as they are celebrated.

Much of what the bishops hoped to achieve through their document of December 4, 1963, began to be realized in this country on November 29, 1964, when the word of the sacraments was largely rendered in English speech.

Speech is the great sacramental sign, of course. Not only is it God's own word (when it is scriptural, and in the other ways He speaks to us); it is also that intelligible sign which removes the confusions that can very easily arise over other kinds of signs. The question is asked: "Yes, but why is the water being poured?" or "What is that application of olive oil supposed to mean?" The sign of the word added to the sign of the sacrament (thing and action) explains what is happening. Take, for example: "I baptize you in the name of the Father and of the Son and of the Holy Spirit" and "I sign you with the sign of the cross, and I confirm you with the chrism of salvation, in the name of the Father and of the Son and of the Holy Spirit." These formulas specify the exact signification of water, of the bishop's hand upraised, now.

A little boy said to his mother one day (the priest had begun to face the people in offering Mass in that parish): "Mother, what is the priest eating and drinking up there?" You see, the boy had been let in on half the sign. If he had heard the words of consecration he would have learned the other half, for they say quite clearly what the priest is eating and drinking.

God is He who, by definition, cannot be comprehended, so much is He beyond us. If He is to make Himself known to us, it must be through a human way of knowing. We could not understand Him in any other way.

Therefore, He employs happenings, gestures, words—all of them symbols of Himself—to communicate with us. The greatest of these signs is His son, Jesus of Nazareth, whom St. Augustine calls "the sacrament of God."

It is through Jesus Christ that the reality of God and His dealings with us manage to come through to us. He is the Word of God, the image of the eternal Father. At the same time, He is a man of our race. All that He said and did in the flesh as a sharer in our manhood are symbols through which we know God. Jesus is in Himself the complete expression of God's communication with us men.

A knowledge of Jesus, you can see, is terribly important if we are to understand the sacraments. Yet, conversely, we cannot get to know Jesus well without a knowledge of the sacraments, those "signs which also instruct."

The *Constitution on the Sacred Liturgy* is wonderfully sound in its sacramental doctrine. Here is why we say that. It devotes one whole chapter out of seven (Articles 47–58) to "The Most Sacred Mystery of the Eucharist." The "Other Sacraments and Sacramentals"—*all* of them, mind you, from baptism to blessings—get but one chapter. (Articles 59–82) Of the latter, seven articles are given to baptism. There is one each on confirmation, penance, and ordination rites. Three articles are concerned with the "last rites," and two have to do with matrimony.

This means that the Council fathers, while committed to the seven sacraments because of their Catholic faith, know very well that there are degrees of importance within that family of seven. The eucharist is the chief sacrament, both because this sacrificial meal contains Him who *is* our salvation, and because the other six have their existence as saving signs in relation to the central one. The Lord established it as *the* memorial of His blessed passion, resurrection from the abode of the dead, and ascension to the glory of heaven.

If the Council fathers had spent an equal amount of time on all seven sacraments, or hadn't put baptism—the gateway to eucharistic life in Christ—in the number two position, we would really have something to worry about. Happily, the bishops went about their work in masterful fashion. By putting the "other sacraments and sacramentals" in one chapter, and interweaving the treatment of sacramentals at that (Articles 60, 62, 63, 79), they reminded us of the long history of *sacramenta maiora* and *sacramenta minora*.

These sacraments and sacramentals, as we call them, were so intertwined for a thousand years that it was only in the twelfth century that a definitive list of seven sacraments emerged. The "sacraments of initiation"—baptism, confirmation, and the eucharist—always had a favored position over the other four, and still do.

Also, it is quite impossible to think of sanctification through the greater signs (the big seven, that is) apart from the use, on the same occasions, of the lesser signs. Think, for example, of all the blessings, invocations, and gestures that go to make up the Mass, or a baptismal service, or a wedding. It is unthinkable that the great sign—the exchange of consents in marriage, for example, or the canon of the Mass which changes the bread and wine—could go unaccompanied by a whole host of lesser rites and still have its full impact.

Theologians have engaged in some very doubtful theology about sacramentals over the years, all of which the *Constitution* buries by its discreet silences.

There was, for example, the notion which flourished for

quite a while which said that the sign value of a sacramental depended entirely on whether you understood it or not (take a blessing, or a blessed object like palm or ashes), whereas the essence of a sacrament was that it "worked" in any case, provided you didn't hinder its action by your sinfulness. This explanation was well-intentioned enough, but, in its attempt to describe the sacraments as superior signs, it ended by saying that it didn't much matter whether you got their message as signs at all—just so long as you "fulfilled the conditions"!

Another difference you often hear (and there is much more truth at the base of this distinction) is that the seven sacraments give or restore divine life whereas the lesser signs serve only to stir up holy thoughts and dispositions in us. In other words, the first group of seven signs *causes* sanctifying grace in us, whereas the larger family of sacramentals serves as the *occasion* for the conferring of actual graces, that is, the passing helps that God gives us to resist temptation or come closer to Him in love.

The only trouble with that explanation is that it is so neat it doesn't sufficiently account for the considerable number of sacramentals that are to be found throughout a well-celebrated or well-administered sacrament. Does a blessing or an exorcism have one way of acting when it is part of a sacrament and another when it is not? Is it true to say that sacraments have an effect of themselves and apart from the Church, whereas sacramentals do not cause grace of themselves, but only through the Church?

If you read the *Constitution* with care, you will see how it avoids these many unresolved theological problems by its careful silences. "Sacraments impart grace," it says, but in addition "the very act of celebrating them most effectively disposes the faithful to receive this grace in a fruitful manner. . . ." (Article 59) Again, sacramentals "bear a resemblance to the sacraments"; they "signify effects, particularly of a spiritual kind, which are obtained through the Church's intercession"; and by them "various occasions in life are rendered holy." (Article 60)

Both of the above two statements are, as they stand, interchangeable for sacraments and sacramentals. The one clear difference in the *Constitution*'s wording is its declaration that by the sacramentals ". . . men are disposed to receive the chief effects of the sacraments." (Article 60) That says that these two families of signs are very closely allied, and that many signs are in the service of a lesser number, namely the seven which have a greater spiritual effect.

You can almost guess the wording of the one article concerned with sacramentals exclusively. It reads: "The sacramentals are to undergo a revision which takes into account the primary principle of enabling the faithful to participate intelligently, actively, and easily; the circumstances of our own day must also be considered. When rituals are revised, as laid down in Article 63, new sacramentals may also be added as the need for these becomes apparent. . . ." (Article 79)

22. Why Can't the Office Be Your Prayer Book?

There used to be prayer books in Catholic circles. Practically speaking, there aren't any published any more except as parts of missals. How did this come about?

The fate of prayer books is pretty much a development of the "liturgical movement" of the last fifty or sixty years, coupled with the restlessness of the age. People don't sit still long enough to pray in private the way they used to. Even more to the point, the liturgy has been disclosed to them as primarily a holy *action*. It has its contemplative moments, of course, but in it contemplation is induced by action. Prayer books, old style, are chiefly concerned with silent, contemplative prayer.

This gives us a clue as to why resistance to participation in the liturgy is so fierce in some quarters. The Mass had long been celebrated throughout the Western world as an *action* by the priest but as a *contemplation* by the people. All of a sudden, it has lately been identified as an action by the people as well and thereby a contemplation for all. If people haven't been slowly prepared for this over many decades—or even over the two decades since Pope Pius XII wrote his encyclical letter *On the Sacred Liturgy* in 1947—you can hardly blame them for their annoyance. They feel somehow duped, taken in, in the Church that is their own household. It is as if someone had changed the rules without even taking a voice vote from the dues-paying members.

One hopes that this unhappiness and even resentment will be reduced in time by programs of parish education in the liturgy. Meanwhile, no one in the Church may lose sight of the fact that individual, silent prayer—often contemplative in nature—has an age-old home in Catholic life. The *Constitution on the Sacred Liturgy* has some reminders on the need we all have to "pray to the Father in secret" and without ceasing.

(See Matthew 6, 6 and 1 Thessalonians 5, 17, both cited in Article 12.) The apostolate of suffering and simple endurance —"the cross"—is spoken of in the same article.

Immediately afterwards, mention is made of popular devotions, especially those of long standing, which are ordered by the apostolic see (the divine praises at benediction would be an example of this), or encouraged in "individual churches" (meaning dioceses and countries). The latter are to be fostered by national hierarchies where possible. (See Article 13.) Any such devotions, however (for example, Miraculous Medal or Sorrowful Mother services or a novena of grace), "should be so drawn up that they harmonize with the liturgical seasons, accord with the sacred liturgy, are in some fashion derived from it, and lead the people to it, since, in fact, the liturgy by its very nature far surpasses any of them." (Article 13)

That kind of adaptation to the liturgy of the season is already being attempted in some Catholic circles. It takes long, hard work, but most of all, deep biblical knowledge and a conviction that the bishops are absolutely serious in this directive of theirs.

We said above that the liturgy of the Mass is chiefly an action allowing for contemplative behavior within its structure. We should immediately point out the long-standing Christian custom of praying at other times of the day in the spirit of the day's eucharistic celebration. This contemplative exercise is called "the divine office." It, too, sometimes has the character of a public celebration. A monastery church filled with monks or friars or a convent chapel of nuns is the scene of the daily recitation of hymns, psalms, and other Scripture readings and selections from the Fathers.

The practice is thought so important by the Council fathers that they devote one entire chapter out of seven to it in their *Constitution*. (See Chapter IV, containing Articles 83–101); there are nineteen articles in all, compared to the twenty-four articles devoted to the six sacraments other than the Mass, and sacramentals.) The divine office must mean a lot to the Church to receive all that attention from her bishops.

Up until now, the office has had a special meaning for the

clergy of the West and those "choir religious" who recite the office as part of their rule.

It could be that with large populations able to read as never before in the world's history the office has a great future as the prayer book of ordinary Christians. When we are reminded that God's Son, "taking human nature, introduced into his earthly exile that hymn which is sung throughout all ages in the halls of heaven" (Article 83), it occurs to us that "his Church, which is ceaselessly engaged in praising the Lord and interceding for the salvation of the whole world" is not a Church of priests and religious only.

Maybe if the office is revised in a way suited to the active lives of priests and teaching brothers and sisters it will at the same time be equally suitable for all sorts of adult Christians. Any who engage in this prayer, says the *Constitution*, "are standing before God's throne in the name of the Church, their Mother." (Article 85)

The first requirement for making the office your prayer book is that it be related to your daily life. It must be in ordinary, good English. It can't have a black cover, gold edges, and ribbons (RIBBONS!) or you'll never pull it out of your pocket on a commuter train. It must look and read like an ordinary book.

The "two hinges on which the daily office turns" are morning prayer, Lauds, and evening prayer, Vespers. These are the chief hours and are always to be thought of as such. (See Article 89.) A suitable night prayer, Compline, is fine, too. (See Article 89b.) Matins makes sense as a prayer for pre-dawn recitation in religious houses, but other people ought to read or pray it anytime they get the chance. The big difference between this prayer and the first three we mentioned is that they are to be made up chiefly of the psalms, whereas Matins is more fittingly composed of other longer readings. (See Article 89c.)

A last detail proposed in the *Constitution* for the reform of the divine office is that the prayer called Prime, which used to come right next to the community Mass, should be dropped. Of the brief prayers said at three-hour intervals throughout the day (Terce, Sext, and None, originally scheduled for

9 A.M., 12 noon, and 3 P.M.), only one is to be chosen to bridge the gap between morning and evening prayer by those who don't live according to a regular religious schedule. (See Articles 89d and e.)

The changes contained in the paragraph immediately above have gone into effect already, so far as secular priests are concerned. Those men in holy orders who say the office privately can receive permission to pray it in English (Article 101), and many of them now do so. Religious men and nuns (not sisters) must say the whole office; they can't leave out those two shorter hours. (Article 95a) And religious men who are clerics are still unable to pray the office in common in their own language. (See Article 101, which "doesn't say yes and doesn't say no," but, by what it doesn't say, seems to mean "no.")

This whole discussion could be a dreadful bore to you if you don't have any plans to "hie thee to a nunnery" or to ask some benign bishop to lay hands on you in ordination. The point of it all is this: Must daily prayer in a liturgical spirit be confined to a handful of professionals forever? There's no reason why it should be. In fact, the whole spirit of the *Constitution* is against two kinds of Christianity, one for the "red team," the pros, and the other for the "blue team," the amateurs. Yet this spirit is very much with us at present. What can bring it to an end?

The transition whereby the Bible becomes every Catholic's possession will deal the deathblow to this pro and amateur distinction. If only people could get to know the psalms, really know them, they would want to pray the psalms. But the Mass liturgy in English, along with its extensive hymn-singing, is already beginning to achieve this. Secondly, people will give private prayer a chance—or public prayer said privately, which is what this is—if they are provided with something sane, solid, and socko, not a collection of "wouldst vouchsafe" and "O, anguishing, languishing" type prayers.

That's why the present writer, who is a secular priest, looks forward to a first-class revision of the divine office. Once it was revised, it could be given to any layman who shows a taste for prayer, on the theory that his or her Christian life is just like mine. At the moment, I'm still busy pretending I'm a monk after twenty-two years of reading those prayers.

And the ribbons! I don't know two men in this world I'd dare to give a book with ribbons to.

23. The Shape of a Year of Salvation

If you were to pick up a book of Jewish scholarship, you would shortly discover that 1965 had C.E. after it rather than A.D. And if the writer wished to speak of the death of Alexander the Great, he would say it happened in the year 323 B.C.E., not 323 B.C.

What's the difference?

Basically, Jesus of Nazareth is the difference.

Since He is "Lord" for those who believe in Him, they do not hesitate to say that they are reading a book produced "anno Domini (in the year of the Lord) 1965." Then there is a switch from Latin to English, as one says of Alexander the Great that he died on June 13, 323 B.C., "before Christ." That testifies to the widespread belief that Jesus of Nazareth is the Christ, or using the Hebrew word instead of the Greek, that He is the Messiah.

Not everyone who says or writes "B.C." believes that Jesus is the Christ, but this way of reckoning the years has been in use ever since the Roman Empire toppled and Christianity won out politically. (The Romans used to figure their dates "from the founding of the city," namely Rome: "a.u.c.," or "ab urbe condita.")

But back to Jewish writers who have a firm conviction that Jesus is neither Lord nor Christ. They solve their delicate problem in conscience by calling this year 1965 C.E., "Common Era." In the same way, they would say that poor Alexander was taken of a fever in 323 B.C.E., "Before the Common Era."

For Christians, each year is not only a "year of salvation" (it is the same for Jews, of course—their Savior being Yahweh, the God of Israel), but, in particular, it is a year of salvation through Jesus whom the Father has constituted Savior of the world. God, in raising Him up from the dead, has made Him Lord and Messiah. It is through faith in Him that we live.

Our Lord lived and died and rose in history: time past. We are delivered from the power of sin and death likewise in history: time present. We are headed toward life in eternity: not time future but a timeless condition. Jesus Christ, through whom we are saved, is at this moment reigning in heaven, which is not a place as Vienna is a place but a timeless condition which we call eternity.

Still, as yet we know nothing by way of experience of eternity. The earth is our home. Time is our familiar element. Salvation for us is something that is being accomplished in our lives over a span of years. Each year in the earthly lifetime of a Christian—or indeed of any man, whether he has heard the gospel preached or not—is a year of salvation.

The *Constitution on the Sacred Liturgy* of Vatican II devotes one entire chapter out of seven—namely chapter five—to "The Liturgical Year." That chapter title is another way of saying "The Year of Celebration" or the way in which we come to possess salvation over the course of a year.

Now, the historical event that gives us life is the paschal mystery. But we die and rise with Christ *now*, not by harking back in memory to the year 30 A.D. The deed that makes salvation contemporaneous with us and with men of every age is the present-day celebration of the paschal mystery. It happens in our lifetimes, on our Easters, on every Sunday and feast day of our years on the earth. Every sacrament contains and unfolds the paschal mystery in some way, as does all of Scripture, but the Mass is that heart and center of the sacramental universe which shows forth the mystery of Christ best.

Even though every Lord's day commemorates the Lord's resurrection, which is also memorialized annually on the Feast of Easter, the Church within the cycle of a year "unfolds the whole mystery of Christ, from the incarnation and birth until the ascension, the day of Pentecost, and the expectation of blessed hope and of the coming of the Lord." (*Constitution*, Article 102) The powers of Christ and His merits in the order of grace are thereby made available to me. They are "in some way made present for all time." (Article 102)

Every Catholic knows about the feasts of Mary: her assumption, immaculate conception, and the others. They are basically feasts of her Son to whom she "is joined by an inseparable bond." (Article 103) Our Lady is an image of all we hope to be. We are redeemed by Christ's death and resurrection as she is, and we celebrate the feasts of Mary, greatest of the saints, to remind ourselves of all that it is our calling to become.

The annual cycle of the martyrs and other saints has the same purpose. With the feast of each of them, there is proclaimed a new passage from death to life in Christ. A saint is a person who is a new example to us of the image of Jesus. Through the saints, the Church pleads to God for our needs. (See Article 104.)

The last element that goes to make up the liturgical year is the recurring instruction, prayer, and works of penance and mercy which we are familiar with from keeping Lent and the other ember days and vigils. (See Article 105.)

The *Constitution* could have made Easter central in the liturgical year and developed the celebration of Sunday and all the feasts from that day. Instead, it chose to make the Sunday, any Sunday, its starting point: "the foundation and kernel of the whole liturgical year." (Article 106) Every other celebration, "unless it be of the greatest importance," must yield to Sunday.

It is of primary concern to remove this weekly observance from the realm of mere routine. The regular recurrence of Sunday, not to speak of the precept which requires our presence at Mass on this day, can easily deaden interest in this major event. ". . . It should be proposed to the piety of the faithful and taught to them so that it may become in fact a day of joy . . ." (Article 106)

This means a lot of work ahead for parents, parish priests, and educators. Sunday Mass is so widely identified in Catholic thought as something one must be present at "under pain of mortal sin," and is so little considered in terms of actively begetting us " 'through the resurrection of Jesus Christ from the dead, unto a living hope' (1 Pet. 1, 3)" (*ibid.*), that a whole new mentality regarding it must be fostered. Already, Sunday Mass is being rivaled by a thousand things like sleep and sports and relaxation. It must become a matter of interest and concern for Christians *in itself*, not because of any serious obligation that attends it.

Much has been done in the last year or so to carry out the requirements of Article 106. People are beginning to have insights into how the Mass celebrates their redemption through the improved character of the reading and the preaching, the common recitation, and the song. They find themselves wanting to be at Mass in a way they didn't before. And they begin to feel strangely left out at communion time because it is becoming so clear that the Mass is a meal more than it is anything else.

All this is the result of an increased awareness of what it means to "come together into one place so that, by hearing the word of God and taking part in the eucharist, they may call to mind the passion, the resurrection, and the glorification of the Lord Jesus. . . ." (Article 106)

Many of the things we do in the Roman liturgy are connected with the agricultural life of Europe where the cycle of feasts and saints' days developed. Basically, of course, the pattern was set in Palestine, which has a spring very much like ours. Now, just because there isn't any grain grown on the tundra or because the Eskimos don't drink wine, we don't have to turn our backs on the relation of the liturgy to nature altogether. You feel a little foolish, though, keeping the rogation days (spring prayers for good crops) on West Madison Street in Chicago, or taking part in a Corpus Christi procession in downtown Akron—a procession that used to go great on the Bavarian countryside.

The Council fathers say, "Forget it." Keep the customs of the place, if there are such customs, but make adaptations to the conditions of modern times where necessary. (See Article 107.) Above all else, concentrate on the feasts of the Lord in preference to saints' days (see Article 108), the document counsels. It doesn't speak of feasts of our Lady, who often is put in the embarrassing position of being the chief rival of her Son.

The last part of the treatment of the liturgical year is all about Lent and the sacred three days it leads up to. The Catholic world is reminded that, historically, Lent is a preparation for baptism. (See Article 109.) Many of its features are quite meaningful if their baptismal character is brought out; otherwise, they signify nothing in particular. Therefore, these features are to be restored whenever possible.

The penances of Lent are not simply a matter of doing hard things because Jesus suffered for us. They are a reminder to the whole Christian community of the social consequences of sin. For that reason, these penitential exercises must have a social character and not an individual character only. The whole Church does penance in Lent, and through these penances it prays to God for sinners. The latter are no less members of the Church because they are sinners. In fact, their chief hope as sinners is that they are members of the Church; this means they have brothers to pray and do penance in their behalf. (See Articles 109 and 110.)

As this chapter comes to an end, the writer is reminded strongly by the content of the final article of Chapter V (Article 111) of a research study he directed recently on Christian life in rural areas of the Philippines. Relics and statues are terribly important in the people's lives there. There is almost no consciousness of the paschal mystery compared with their concern with this or that patron saint, this procession or that shrine in the corner of one's household. As the reading continued—it was done by a Filipino research student who had a great concern for the liturgy—one had the feeling, "How badly these populations need instruction!"

Then the thought occurred that in our own country people are in a similar condition of need. Many parishioners at present find it nearly impossible to distinguish between one liturgical season and another. The year is "flattened out" completely by the way the feasts are celebrated—or not celebrated. Careful study and serious attention to the character of the Sunday, the feast, or the season are the only ways to improve things.

And the almost daily Mass for the dead in some parishes is the greatest enemy of all. Next to it, life in the rural Philippines is a paradise of Christian enlightenment.

24. The Church that Sings Together Clings Together

It's pretty important to know what the folk-singing craze means on the national scene, for if we gain some insight into its significance we'll know considerably more about what singing in church means—or can mean.

The subject is a complex one. "Folk singing" in its purest sense probably means ballads of the Burl Ives-Joan Baez-Pete Seeger type. The songs they sing often tell a story you're able to follow. Even when that isn't the case, there is usually a beauty or refinement of speech about the lyrics which makes you realize you're in the presence of some good poetry.

Most of the better American folk songs came from England or Scotland to the hill country of Ohio, Kentucky, and Tennessee, or to the Ozark Mountains of Arkansas and Missouri. Many of them had been sung in the English midlands and Scottish highlands, or in Ireland, for years before they crossed the ocean. And, of course, a few good ones of high quality have been written lately, like "If I Had a Hammer" and "Blowing in the Wind."

There is another entire family of tunes which is a cousin to folk music. It is usually called mountain music or country music. It, too, has a cousin, cowboy music.

The best known "relative" of American folk music in the United States is the music that comes from the West Indies: places like Jamaica, Trinidad, and Barbados. We know it for two reasons. Many people from those islands come up to the United States and sing it here (like Harry Belafonte). Besides, it's in English which makes it easier for us to sing it.

The North American continent has many other kinds of folk music: that of the French Canadian settlers, for example, of the Irish, Polish, and Greek communities, which one hears on the local radio stations of larger cities, and also the folk tunes of Mexico, Puerto Rico, and Cuba.

Musicologists say that the only native American music is the Negro spiritual—along with its offshoot, jazz.

Now, all these strands reveal something important if you weave them together. They establish that the United States, which, for so long, was described as unmusical and without any tradition of its own in song, is now exploding in outbursts of melody. The only drawback is that many people feel that what is emerging as the popular mode of American song is not very melodious!

This means that, although we are becoming a singing people, we are in danger of falling into a debased tradition of song. If an entire nation has very few good examples of a pure melodic line or of good harmonies in two, three, or four parts, its people will naturally sing in the way they know when they come together in church. They will drag things out sorrowfully or hop along in rabbity style or else do a little bit of both.

Worst of all, they will grow progressively unfamiliar with the good work that has been done in choral song in the past—not that they must always sing out of the past, but they must have good "musical memories" if the future is to be bright. We should not wish to descend to the lowest level of popular culture when we sing in church. Rather, we should really intend to raise our hearts to God through raising our voices. The point is it may not work out that way, so strong is the tidal wave of the familiar. And the familiar is pretty bad.

All these elements are of utmost importance in exploring the meaning of Chapter VI of the *Constitution on the Sacred Liturgy,* "Sacred Music."

Perhaps the most significant part of the liturgical renewal in the United States is the assumption that song by the people must be part of any celebration. It really is a marvel that in most American dioceses the key role of song has been taken for granted. Yet this factor is likewise the greatest potential threat to the success of liturgical restoration.

How can it be both at the same time?

It is quite simple. When an important thing is done well, the whole effort goes forward in giant steps. When it is done badly, the crippling effect on the total enterprise is indescribable. But music in general and song in particular are at the heart of any true expression of religious conviction. They not only express it; they help to increase it.

When people have been praying publicly without music for years, their first reaction to the introduction of any music whatever is resentment—simply because it means an end to silence. (By now, you see, silence has come to equal "prayer" for them.)

If, however, the quiet of the Mass is replaced by melodious congregational song and good choir work, most people will welcome that change in very short order. If a shoddy rendition of poor hymns is substituted for a satisfying hour of silence in the midst of a noisy life, then congregational singing will become the worst enemy of all. Finally, if large populations get to enjoy bad hymns, sung as wretchedly as they deserve to be sung, we will be in a decline in our corporate prayer lives like the cultural decline we are in now.

Sacred music needs to be "connected with the liturgical action" if it is to be considered holy. (Article 112) That means that Mary-hymns on the feast of Corpus Christi are out of place and "real-presence" songs have no place during the preparation of the gifts. Much more to the point, the complete rendition of a people's chant like the "Glory to God," or "Holy, Holy, Holy" by a choir is unconnected with the liturgical action because the people are being robbed of their role.

Before, the priest or a choir did the people's task for them. Now they need to recover their function, just as choirs, in turn, need to do difficult pieces that ordinary congregations cannot do (for example, the alternate verses of the creed or "Lamb of God" in polyphonic style, or motets beyond the ability of the people to sing—but not to enjoy—while the eucharist is being distributed).

It is quite wrong to squander our treasury of sacred music from the past, the *Constitution* says. (Article 114) Only the continuation of a class of lovers of Church music can see to it that we do not do that. That is why bishops and pastors are earnestly charged with fostering choirs while at the same time they must have a serious concern for congregational song.

Now here is where the real trouble begins. The Catholic Church in America has never had a great tradition of church music. This was true before the recent liturgical changes, and the changes, if anything, only highlighted this painful fact. Our choirmasters and our organists haven't been well enough trained or well enough paid. Expecting them to form congregations musically in light of this economic situation is unrealistic. There is, besides, a direct relation between feeling secure at a skill, "on top of it," as it were, and the ease with which advice about change is received. Many church musicians are too insecure musically to take in a new approach to their task with equanimity.

At the present time there is a whole country full of generous, self-sacrificing, underpaid Church musicians—many of them not very skilled—who are being told by people who know even less about music than they (or a good deal more, which, in the circumstances, is worse), that they must cease and desist from their cadenzas and accompany the people in the singing of hymns.

Lots of these musicians, as a result, think of the liturgy as a conspiracy against their persons, and of "liturgists" as a class of wicked men vowed to their destruction. Nothing could be further from the truth. *Yet this is the way things are bound to appear until competent leaders of song begin to work closely with good organists.* Until that day, the ragged rendering of hymns by congregations which have no director is bound to increase annoyance on every side, and possibly to threaten programs of participation with extinction.

The *Constitution* asks for some important reforms in seminaries and houses of religious formation in the teaching and practice of music. (See Article 115.) That's realistic enough. Otherwise, the parish clergy and school staffs will prove a hindrance rather than a help in working with musically skilled lay people or musicians employed by the Church who know a great deal more than they.

The plea for retaining Gregorian chant in Article 116 is realistic if the Roman liturgy remains a Latin-language affair in its entirety. This promises to remain the case almost nowhere, not even in monasteries. The updating of musical tastes and needs is taken care of by the phrase "other things being equal." It is said in this context that the chant should be "given pride of place in liturgical services." A few things aren't by any means equal, namely the vowel quality of English words as contrasted with Latin, and the detail of the lapse of ten centuries since some of the chants were written.

Strong encouragement is given to countries and cultures to weave their own musical traditions into the liturgy. (See Article 119.) The fact that the phrase "especially mission lands" occurs there does not mean that only they have the problem. In a sense, the cultures that are most developed musically cry out for this adaptation more than any others. There is nothing so discouraging to the trained musician as the assumption that there are freedoms at the ends of the earth that he somehow does not enjoy. (There are some musicians, of course, who want the phrase with a passion to describe the bongo-drum set only.)

Composers are encouragingly told that their vocation is to increase the store of the treasures of sacred music. (See Article 121.) They must attend to the needs of large choirs, small choirs, and the "entire assembly of the faithful." Very much to the point, the words to the melodies must either be the texts of the liturgy themselves or be drawn from biblical sources or be great expressions of Christian faith. (See Article 121.) There is a "moon-June-soon" pattern in sacred music that goes: "divine-benign-sublime" (and we do mean that last jarring assonance). Being more doggerel than dogma it works against any attempt to raise the mind and heart to God.

If a field has gone untended for years and years, how can it be made to yield a good harvest? Ploughing, irrigation, fertilizer—none of those things can be omitted. But most of all there is need of a clever farmer. Good men and materials come high. You have to pay good sums for them.

All of which is to say we will never have good music in the liturgy until we're ready to pay the price!

25. Art for God's Sake – or Men's Sake?

When that Metro-Goldwyn-Mayer lion comes on the screen and snarls at us (maybe he's seen the picture?), the motto on the great seal of M-G-M–which Leo is smack in the middle of–says *"Ars Gratia Artis."* That isn't Sam Goldwyn's reply to "United Artis'." It means "Art for art's sake."

Who then is Art?

He must be the company's treasurer.

All of us have, I think, a pretty good idea of what that motto means. The art object has a glory all its own. Its very existence is its justification.

A canvas or a carving or casting in bronze isn't geared to any practical purpose. It "says" what the artist is dreaming. If he dreams great dreams, there's more beauty in the world than there was–that's all. He has enriched the lives of thousands.

A work of art can't help reflecting in some way the infinite beauty of God. Every human product is a sign of Him. If it has as its special aim being set aside for use in divine worship, it "should be truly worthy, beautiful, and becoming." It should be "a sign and symbol of the supernatural world," that world of grace that is all around us and in heaven too.

The *Constitution on the Sacred Liturgy* optimistically says that "The Church has been particularly careful to see that sacred furnishings should worthily and beautifully serve the dignity of worship." (Article 122) Somebody's thinking wishfully! The Church hasn't been too careful about beauty in the fifty states of this federal republic (to take but one example). She has been careless in Paris, offhanded in Rome, and downright negligent in certain countries that don't bear naming now.

Holy Church, the earthly Jerusalem, has, in a word, ugly churches everywhere.

What then do the Council fathers mean? They mean to speak a truth, which is that over the twenty centuries Christian men have brought into existence some buildings and objects of great beauty in the service of God. Taking the Church fully, that is, all those people who go to make her up, it is undeniable that "Holy Mother Church has always been the friend of the fine arts and has ever sought their ennobling assistance." (Article 122)

Often "the Church" will have been artists themselves, from whom the clergy did not especially wish to receive a contribution. At times "the Church" meant churchmen like the bishops and abbots who erected great temples such as Notre Dame de Paris or the cathedral in Salisbury. And we may not forget the great mass of Christian people who by appreciating good art and thus passing a correct estimate on it were the most important friends of the fine arts.

Since artistic relevance is always tied to cultures, there is no single "great art" that can serve as an absolute. Every age and way of life will be marked by materials, style, or ornamentation proper to it. This will normally be prompted by the progress of the technical arts with the passage of time.

Perhaps the most forceful declaration of the Council fathers on art is the one with which Article 123 begins: "The Church does not have any particular style of art as her own." It is really quite shocking to visit far-off places like India and there discover a Christian church that looks for all the world like the central edifice of an Italian or Spanish town. We've got Ireland-in-Korea, France-in-Thailand, and gingerbread-Rococo-all-over-the-place.

The theory is that "the Church . . . has admitted styles from every period according to the natural talents and circumstances of peoples, and the needs of the various rites." (Article 123) That's good theory. It's what has sometimes been done that causes the pain. Art belongs in the culture that produced it, not in the midst of another culture.

Every race and region has made its own contribution, the *Constitution* says in the same paragraph. The artistic reality is twofold: the art proper to the present age, and the treasury of art which has accumulated over the centuries. The latter "must be carefully preserved." The former "must be given free scope in the Church." Only by such a delicate balance can we have any assurance that our buildings will be adorned and our rites clothed with due reverence and honor. Only then will sight and sound sing a chorus of praise to the eternal Father in tones which echo the Church's faith.

Frequently simplicity, not ornateness, is the key to beauty. "Sumptuous display" is the demon of the piece according to the *Constitution.* (See Article 124.) Like the shopgirl who said she wanted "seagrams" on her wedding veil, Christians often have a chips-with-everything mentality. "When in doubt sprinkle gold."

Oscar Levant said once, "I've lived in Hollywood for years, and it's true there's lots of false tinsel there. But believe me, behind that false tinsel there's real tinsel." That describes a lot of Church art.

The worst of it is that poor art usually costs more. You can get fine art at good prices because the best artists haven't yet been corrupted by money. The machine-finished carvings or the grimly regular glass panes of Sig. Dott. Azzecca Garbugli or Atélier Beaugrosgrand Frères make a pastor and his people pay *per il naso.* Meanwhile, in the same city, Mr. Frank Higgins or Mr. Albert Schmidt is busy doing wrought-iron artistry that people are coming from Oslo to see.

This isn't a "Buy American" pitch. Far from it. It is the expression of an earnest desire to think along with the Council fathers. They propose that they themselves, by the encouragement and favor they show to artists, should strive after noble beauty "in art which is truly sacred," including vestments and the adornments of churches. Works that are "repugnant to faith, morals, and Christian piety should be removed from churches." (Article 124) Notice, it doesn't say works that Christian people like, but works that don't accord with the Church's faith. That means anything false, cheap, or flashy. The bishops use some pretty strong terms here: "depraved forms . . . lack of artistic worth, mediocrity and pretense."

But, of course, this is a program that must proceed slowly, and by way of both popular education and patronage of the

arts. It cannot go well by virtue of terse directives to pastors to "tear down that shrine." A merely negative attitude in these matters is called iconoclasm. What is needed is positive appreciation of the place of the arts in the sacramental prayer lives of the faithful.

You don't find any blanket condemnation in the *Constitution* of statues or paintings or icons. Their veneration by the faithful is to be maintained. Nevertheless, "their number should be moderate and their relative positions should reflect right order." (Article 125) The bishops' reason for the last prohibition is important: ". . . otherwise they may create confusion among the Christian people and foster devotion of doubtful orthodoxy."

Not everyone knows what it is that constitutes truly sacred art, and this the bishops are quick to point out. They say that the bishops in charge of sees "shall give a hearing to the diocesan commission on sacred art and, if needed, also to others who are especially expert. . . ." (Article 126) Practically speaking, the only persons who should serve on such commissions are qualified art critics and men who know the requirements of the liturgy, not working artists. The latter are in search of contracts and commissions in the field of Church art as any other practitioner is. If they become a jury passing judgment on fellow professionals, they are immediately disqualified from trying to get any work in that diocese on the principle that "no one is a fit judge of his own case."

It is quite the same with members of diocesan music commissions. No composer or publisher should be allowed to serve as a commission member, for immediately he will find himself in an intolerable "conflict of interest" situation. The person learned in art and music who is not, at this point in his career, engaged in creating any works of art is the one best qualified to serve.

If you read of the tremendous care taken in the Eastern Church to form religiously and theologically those men who produce icons—sacred images painted on wood—you will have some notion of the holy burden bishops place on themselves in Article 127. "Bishops should have a special concern for artists, so as to imbue them with the spirit of sacred art and of

the sacred liturgy." They may do this in person or through
suitable priests who love art and know it. Academies or
schools of sacred art should also be set up in various places
around the world for this purpose.

Artists need help in recalling the sacredness of their work
of fostering the piety of the faithful and contributing to their
religious formation. Similarly, bishops and priests who commission art pieces need to be reminded of the integrity of
genius and the legitimate demands of art.

It's all very complicated, but that is no reason to keep us
from getting on with the job. One problem is that many of the
Church's laws on the shape and construction of altars, the
baptistery and sanctuary furnishings, reflect the human needs
and cultures of the past rather than of the present and future.
Revise these laws, says Article 128, along with the revision of
the liturgical books. (See also Article 25.)

In the myth, Procrustes cut off hands, arms, feet, heads,
when his guests didn't fit in his bed. The situation of today is
that there still remain requirements of Church law that accord ill with the needs of Christian people at worship. The
Constitution says: "Change them."

26. Building Churches to Be Prayed In

Belfast in Northern Ireland has a handsome new airport. So does Mexico City. Brussels Airport is a fine one, likewise Dulles in Virginia, and those in New Orleans, Memphis, Atlanta, and Chicago. The John F. Kennedy Airport in New York is like five, not one—all of them breathtaking. That list may not be entirely satisfactory, for if any building isn't on a par with the others, the point is lost.

The point is that these are such fine expressions of the human spirit that they deserve to be churches.

Sometimes you hear it said of an exciting new church: "You can't tell it from a supermarket—or a bank." Now, if all supermarkets were ugly and all banks repulsive that remark would say something. But in fact they are not. The banks and supermarkets that figure in that comparison, one fears, are not the unsightly ones (which are many) but the prize-winning ones (which are few). They tend to look quite a lot like the prize-winning churches (which are few but not as few as they used to be).

There is a fairly widespread sentiment that none of these modern churches should get a prize. Despite this sentiment, men of taste keep awarding prizes to the architects and pastors of such churches!

You can tell a church from a supermarket because the people buy food in the one and engage in public prayer in the other.

Banks are for commerce, airports are for waiting, churches are for public worship.

Look to see what's going on in the building. Are people coming and going on airplanes? Are they sitting to hear the word of God and moving forward to eat at the Lord's table? That's what determines whether the building is a church or an airport, not any preconceived notion on what "churchiness" consists in or what the precise character of "airportiness" is. *A building should help you to do well what you're supposed to be doing in it.* If it does this by way of beauty, it is, on all counts, a good building.

It is true, of course, that there has been much confusion on the building scene. Take the buildings in the United States in the last century or even in this. Many of them look like the temples of ancient Greece. A county courthouse *may* resemble the Parthenon, of course; there's no law against it. It's just a question of cultural transplantation and lack of imagination and possible waste of the taxpayers' money. The waste isn't because money is being spent on a fine-looking building. That would be money well spent. The waste of public funds comes with unsuccessful copies and architectural hybrids.

Stanford White patterned the Pennsylvania Station in New York on the Baths of the Emperor Caracalla in Rome. Nobody has the right to say: "Copycat!" or "Vulgarizer!" But the architect can be legitimately asked: "When the problem is waiting for trains, do the vaulted ceilings have to rise that high?" Or again, in the case of Greek-temple-like structures where property deeds are filed and birth records kept: "Why should men and women spend the day in those stone dungeons when someone went to the trouble of inventing plate glass?"

Churches have traditionally been dark places, not because God is spooky but because structural steel hadn't been invented yet. You needed all those side walls for the support of high roofs. The great engineering geniuses of the middle ages were the men who let the most light in, not the men who built fortresses to do double duty in case the town were sacked by friendly, neighboring Christians.

It's only third-rate copyists who design dark churches with narrow aisles—the churches that require bus service to the altar rail. No great medieval builder would now construct the kind of church he did then. Assuming he possessed a knowledge of modern construction methods, he would also have a much better grasp of the theology of the Mass and the shape of its rite than he could have had in his own day. Why? Because he was a medieval man, that's why.

Liturgical reform is needed because there has been serious,

centuries-long lack of participation by the people in the Church's worship. Better churches can be built only when that participation begins to be fully restored. That is simply a way of saying that Catholics will get better churches when they begin to take their proper part in public sacramental prayer. Then good churches will be constructed by popular demand.

"When churches are to be built," the *Constitution on the Sacred Liturgy* says, "let great care be taken that they be suitable for the celebration of liturgical services and for the active participation of the faithful." (Article 124)

The suitability of a building for the active participation of congregations means that the people should be able to see the priest and his ministers as they perform the sacred rites, hear them as they read or preach (preferably without mikes), and move freely about when they are not required to kneel or sit.

A choir or "schola" should be fully visible. So should the sound-producing part of an organ. This is partly connected with seeing those people who have special roles to play in worship, but it has more to do with the shape of the human ear. When God starts putting the shell of the ear toward the front of the head it will begin to make some sense to put our skilled musicians at our backs.

In the preceding chapter we hinted at the need to revise or rescind some legislation in the Western Church if architects and pastors are to proceed in complete freedom. Here is the exact wording of that requirement:

"These laws [which need an early revision] refer especially to the worthy and well planned construction of church buildings, the shape and construction of altars, the eminence, position, and safety of the eucharistic tabernacle, the dignity and suitability of the baptistery, the proper ordering of sacred images, embellishments, and vestments. Laws which seem less suited to the reformed liturgy are to be brought into harmony with it, or else abolished; and any which are helpful are to be retained, if already in use, or introduced where they are lacking." (Article 128)

The laws referred to which need abolishing, supplementing, and replacing are found in the Roman missal of the year 1570, the Code of Canon Law of 1918, and the decisions of the

Sacred Congregation of Rites in support of the laws found in those two places.

This work of revision has already begun. First of all, there was the Appendix to Chapter VII of the *Constitution* on "Sacred Art and Sacred Furnishings" which was provided to each of the Council fathers at the second session in 1963. There was issued the instruction, dated September 26, 1964, of the commission for implementing the liturgy. This gets quite specific on how new churches are to be built and old ones remodeled. The whole fifth chapter of this instruction (there are five in all) is devoted to it.

"It is better for the high altar to be constructed away from the wall," Article 91 says, "so that one can move round it without difficulty, and so that it can be used for a celebration facing the people." The altar ought to be the focus of all attention. The sanctuary in which it stands should "allow plenty of room for the ceremonies." If the celebrant's seat is behind the altar, as fittingly it may be to indicate that he is presiding over the whole gathering, it should not give the appearance of being the bishop's throne.

"Side altars are to be few in number. As far as the general shape of the building allows, they should be placed in chapels or in some way cut off from the main body of the church." (Article 93)

You can see from this that the instruction means to bring to an end the confusion between shrines of devotion—which most side altars are—and the eucharistic table which serves for the one sacrifice of a congregation. This fact becomes ever clearer when one reads in Article 94 that candlesticks may be placed near the altar, not on it, if the local bishop approves.

The purpose of this is not merely to achieve a pleasing appearance. The uncluttered altar behind which a priest stands to preside is much more evidently a table for the service of a meal than is the marble slab above which rise successive shelves. Many of our present altars look more like sideboards than dining-room tables, and the Council fathers want to bring this confusion to an end.

Article 95 of the instruction provides that "the most holy eucharist shall be reserved in the solid and inviolable tabernacle placed in the middle of the main altar or of a minor, but truly outstanding, altar. . . ." The same article says: "It is lawful to celebrate Mass facing the people even if there is a tabernacle, small but suitable, on the altar." This is a complete reversal of recent legislation, for until very lately the tabernacle had to be on the main altar. Now it is conceded that Mass can be offered on the main altar *even* if it has a tabernacle.

The instruction makes good provision for a pulpit or two ambos, reading stand or stands. (See Article 96.) The singers and organist must be so arranged that they form part of the congregation. (See Article 97.) The possibility of seeing and hearing "all that is happening in the sanctuary" is insisted upon—"with the assistance of modern technical aids," if necessary. Physical proximity and good acoustics are modern in any age, needless to say! Our technique, at present, is to create hearing problems through the shape of the floor plan and the height of the ceiling or dome, then solve them at high cost with public address systems.

The final article of the instruction of September 26, 1964, requires that the baptistery "lend itself on occasion to the more public administration of the sacrament." This can mean that the font will be in the sanctuary in full view, or in the center as people enter the church, or in a free-standing baptistery.

In February, 1965, the Liturgical Conference in fulfilling its educational role sponsored a seminar in Cleveland for architects and members of diocesan building commissions. It was long overdue—and a great success. The architects and builders were saying: "Tell us how to build." The liturgists were saying: "Be patient. We're just learning how to pray."

27. Which Comes First:
Liturgy or Community?

Perhaps the most important question in the world-wide work of liturgical renewal is the one that will be faced last because it is so hard to solve. There are no easy answers to it. It is this: *Can social structures be so altered that when Christian men assemble for public prayer they will already be a community and not have to depend on the power of Christ in the sacraments to make them one?*

That question may seem, at first, to be based on weak faith in the Savior—in the power of God which He exercises through the Holy Spirit. In fact, though, it describes faith in the divine Three as faith should be experienced. The question does not suppose that God is at work in the world independently of His creatures; it recognizes that He always deals with them in terms of the sorts of creatures they are.

Men are social by nature. There is, of course, a principle at work in their midst that tends to separate them, to drive them apart. That principle is sin. In the form of pride it sets brother against brother, tribe against tribe, nation against nation. The results of sin are evident everywhere—family strife, murder, racial discord, war.

At the same time, there is a power at work in men which tends to draw them together, and that power is stronger than the divisive power of sin. It is stronger because the Creator planted it there, deep in the human heart.

The power we speak of is compounded of a number of things: the bond of flesh by which a man and woman become one person; the bond by which children are a part of the parents who begot them; the need we men have of each other; most importantly, the capability God gives us to love and esteem and cherish one another. All these elements are constantly at work to make us one race, one family of man, one Adam.

Sin is at work to disintegrate this unity but it can never be wholly disintegrated. More than that, God sent His Son as a Second or New Adam to weld the human family into one on better terms than ever before.

Quite apart, for the moment, from the fact of our redemption, it should be pointed out that when human life was more simply organized the divinely authored unifying power at work among us was interfered with less.

We are not dreaming dreams here of the "noble savage" as philosophers of two hundred years ago liked to do. Some of those forerunners of modern scientific sociology had terribly romantic notions. They dreamt of a forest paradise before the whole scheme was corrupted by the "organization" of society.

The fact is that primitive man was badly troubled by a fear of hostile nature, by superstition, by disease, and, of course, by death. Still, he recognized clearly that he was a member of the tribe of X or the people of Y. He did things on a regular rhythm which was strictly governed by the seasons. He did them as a member of a social unit. So much was this the case that it is now known that a man's awareness of being an individual was a development of his earlier awareness that he belonged to a group.

When man waged tribal wars, he was clear about the common cause: his tribe, his people. He had gods that were proper to him alone. The same was true of his sacrifices and incantations. His religion was inseparably a part of his life on the earth. It was a function or aspect of all that he did. Primitive man engaged in public, ritual prayer easily because he had a social identity which cried out to be at peace with the forces that governed his life. Liturgy was easy for him because he already had community. He *was* society, and as society he prayed (or cursed or pleaded).

Things got more complex with the passage of time as everyone knows. There came along in succession agriculture, town life, the city, trade. Through all these developments man managed to keep his social identity by bonds such as language, peoplehood, a relative isolation from other societies, and of course religion. The latter, we repeat, was never separated from the totality of his life. It was the cement that bound together all the rest he did because it dealt in matters that concerned him ultimately.

You can see by simple observation the changes that have been wrought with time. Progress in political life, science, health, and communication have had as their important side effects a fragmenting of the human family. The modern city is huge and complex. People who had stability in their youth one and two generations ago are rootless and alone in their adult years.

The caste system in a great culture like India stays fairly firm, but tribal patterns on the African continent are breaking up rapidly. There is no substitute for them immediately in sight in Africa, as education and technical progress make their influence felt.

Peoples who used to know who they are aren't sure any more. There is, at one and the same time, a new consciousness of national identity and a loss of human identity which will persist until men find their places in the new societies that are coming into being.

You can't turn back the clock of the centuries, God knows. No one wants to, as a matter of fact. But the days and decades and aeons that lie ahead will be marked by an anguished search for community—for those patterns of life together which once made human life richer and fuller, or at the very least endurable.

Take the unit we call the parish. Once it defined all the people who lived in a certain county or shire. Perhaps it was the village that made up the parish. It might have been the southwest segment of a burgeoning city. Everyone in the parish spoke Provençal, or the Irish language, or the Slovenian. They all farmed and traded cattle on market day; they all went down to the sea in ships, or took their sheep up on the slopes to graze. No one had a son off in America, not to speak of a child each in Fort Wayne, San Francisco, and Gabon. On Sunday they went to church (it was the Lord's day, as all knew).

The celebration of Christ's death and resurrection was their way of sanctifying all the rest that they did. The eucharistic meal was the sign of their existence as a community—and as a Christian community. It brought them even further into one. The important thing, though, was that they were already a community when they began to pray. Culturally and socially, they possessed unity. They could build on it. They didn't have to institute a fresh search for unity every Sunday morning.

Now the fact of unity is less and less true in every part of the world. Even this country which has a high degree of cultural homogeneity is marked by important religious differences, by various levels of education, by vastly different outlooks. We have our "haves" and "have nots" including our thirty to fifty million poor. There are painful racial tensions in America and even some leftover strains among national and language groups from immigration days. The melting pot hasn't wholly melted yet—never has, perhaps never will.

Yet the first assumption we go on in Catholic life is that, because all the people in a given geographic area hold the same faith, they comprise one parish, one "little church." They are expected to assemble on a Sunday to pray under Christ's headship as one, even though they are very far from being one on every human question of importance.

Sometimes they are one as a Catholic community but are sharply cut off from the larger community in which they live. They will at times have very little knowledge or sympathy for the Jewish community. They will not have lifted a finger, as a believing and worshiping group, in the interests of civic life, popular education, or community relations. If motivated to do so Catholics could presumably partake in these activities as well as any others. Meanwhile, they keep assembling regularly to *express* community when, in fact, they don't really *possess* community.

The worship of God is a very earthy business. It can't be firmly planted in midair. The reason is that earth is man's home. He is called by God to live a life of brotherhood here, in company with his brothers. This means that he must know his brothers, weep with them, laugh with them. He cannot celebrate the redemption of an abstraction known as *mankind* unless he feels very close to *men.*

The success of liturgical restoration is closely interwoven, don't you see, with social and political action. We can't reasonably pray for peace unless we are working for peace. We can't eat the food of salvation in good conscience so long as anyone goes unfed or unhoused. For the length of time that anyone can't eat and sleep where other men can eat and sleep, our celebrations of the mystery of Christ will ring hollow.

They will be signs of community to which there corresponds no genuine reality of community.

28. The *Constitution* and the Unity of Christians

Whenever we speak about Christian unity, our first concern is with a unity of faith which should flower in mutual charity. Sometimes unity of faith will be incomplete but charity will flourish. One thinks of certain situations where Jews and Christians live in a close relation of love and esteem, but do not worship together because of their differing convictions on how God expects them to express their belief. The opposite situation is the tragic one of a parish or congregation in which everyone professes the same Christian faith while bitter internal differences mar creedal unity, or indeed make a mockery of it.

The Catholic Church is dedicated to unity of faith. It has no commitment to uniformity of practice. The cement of faith is love, not the observance of rules or conduct of worship. This is why the promotion and reform of the liturgy, which is a major expression of the Church's faith, is not being sought through uniformity of liturgical conduct.

There are certain principles and norms which "can and should be applied to the Roman rite and all the other rites," say the world's Catholic bishops.

Article 3 of their *Constitution on the Sacred Liturgy* is the place where they make this observation—speaking, for example, of basics like song in worship, the importance of the central prayer in the eucharistic rite (the canon or anaphora), or the use of the people's language in their public prayer. The same article goes on to say that the "practical norms which follow, however, should be taken as applying only to the Roman rite." There are immediately noted as exceptions those norms which, "in the very nature of things, affect other rites as well."

Thus, the rite in use in Milan, Italy, or Lyons, France, or among the Dominican or Carmelite Fathers, is not destroyed by the action of the Council fathers. All the distinctive gestures, movements, and prayers of these rites remain intact.

The non-Roman Latin rites must all undergo language change, however, and must seek to engage the people fully in participation. Their prayer over the gifts had to be said in a loud voice after the First Sunday in Lent, 1965. The principle of the celebrant's presiding over the "liturgy of the word" from a place somewhat removed from the altar (authorized to begin the same day) is valid for other rites which use Latin, just as much as it is for the Roman rite.

More important in a way is the commitment of all the bishops to liturgical renewal throughout the world and not in the West only. As it happens, it would be extremely unwise at present for Catholics of the Eastern rites to make the slightest change in worship apart from their parent bodies, the Orthodox communions, to which they are historically related. This has happened in the past and the cry has always been: "Westernization!" "Betrayal!" Indeed, the Roman Church at times demanded such modifications of rites as this in proof of "Catholicity." In making these demands the men of the West were quite wrong.

No one can be wrong, however, in issuing a plea that the word of God and the rites that embody it should be comprehensible to the people. After all, an apartment-house dweller in Athens who follows the rite of St. John Chrysostom (or doesn't follow it) is quite as much a modern man as an apartment-house dweller in Rome who prays (or doesn't pray) in the tradition of St. Gregory the Great. Churchmen of the Eastern and Western rites have a similar, proper piety toward their own pasts, but both must remember that the men who pray in them today are not men of the past.

The triumph of Marxism in the Russian revolution of 1917–1919 came about in good part because of the unconcern of the upcoming generation for the ancient prayer forms and patterns of Church organization. The young revolutionaries (seminary trained in some cases, like Stalin) couldn't care less about hour-long litanies and lamps before icons. They discovered that large numbers of educated and professional men were in the same condition of unconcern.

But, of course, the Church should have had then, as in every age, a concern for all men, particularly those who are most influential in a culture. If you stay with the "babushka set" and call it tradition (the matching American phenomenon often lives in suburbia), you can wake up thirty years later and find that you've lost even the babushka (or suburban) crowd. The scientists and thinkers in Russia were on another wave length entirely and by now they've carried the day.

It is the Church's business to be on everybody's wave length. An impossible task? Not at all. The key is unity of faith but not uniformity of practice—no, not even in the same country. Charity is the bond that can bind all together in the one Church of Christ.

The *Constitution* begins by expressing four aims of the Second Vatican Council. The increased vigor of Christian life and adaptation to the needs of the times are the first two. The second two are concerned with unity: "to foster whatever can promote union among all who believe in Christ; to strengthen whatever can help to call the whole of mankind into the household of the Church." (Article 1)

Uniformity of culture or custom is an impossibility; the Council fathers give ample proof that they realize this. In fact, they strongly counsel against any attempts to impose it. (See Articles 37–40, 63–65, 127.) A recurrent phrase in the *Constitution* is "at the discretion of the local ordinary." This means that bishops are encouraged to do different things in their dioceses of the Western Church. It is never supposed, needless to say, that they will go against the legislation which they themselves framed.

Though turning their backs on uniformity, the bishops are forcefully on record in favor of cooperating with the Holy Spirit for Christian and human unity.

The importance of this principle cannot be overstressed. It it not a matter of the wide diversity between Upper Volta and Malaysia, or even between British Columbia and Seine-et-Oise. It touches deeply on the fact that the largest difference between Christians after the split between Orthodoxy and

Rome is the division among heirs of the sixteenth century Reform (Catholic, Anglican, Protestant). Vigorous traditions in worship have developed everywhere. Christians of a Lutheran or Calvinist persuasion have their traditions; Methodists and Baptists have theirs. Even the so-called "nonliturgical" Churches have developed distinctive liturgies, if by this is meant modes of public prayer.

This diversity is by no means regrettable, although the differences in faith which led to it are. The fact is that many Protestant and non-Roman Catholic liturgical formulas can bear a Catholic sacramental meaning, once it is determined what the faith underlying them is. This means that in the reunion of the Churches which all Christians are praying and working for whole communions may be expected to retain their worship forms largely unaltered.

Liturgies are conservative of faith and practice in non-Roman Churches, just as in our own. They often testify to a faith on the part of communicants which is closer to orthodox Catholicity than was the intent of the original framers. This yields to members of these Churches the consoling knowledge that if they come into communion with the Roman Bishop, their faith will be the same as his but their liturgy need not be. Unless their liturgy is marked by words or phrases opposed to Catholic faith, it may very well remain just as it is—provided it gives adequate expression to that faith.

These goals may be distant ones, despite the efforts of the Christians of all the Churches. Probably closer to achievement by far is a series of approaches to unity through the use of common scholarly tools and common prayer, in a liturgical spirit, short of full unity of faith and sacraments.

As the present writer has said elsewhere in print, the *Constitution* "could not have been framed by the Council fathers apart from the contributions made to Christian life and thought by their Anglican and Protestant brothers. Surely our common concern with them over the Bible as the great prayer book of Christians and over meaningful rites and forms will bring us even closer together than in the past."

Already this is coming to pass. Roman Catholic concern with preaching, with hymnody, and with praying the Bible is making an immense difference in ecumenical relations. The Jew need not fear misunderstanding by Catholics nearly so much when Catholics come to see the Jewish roots of their faith and of the liturgy which expresses it. On every side the pain of separation is felt more keenly, once it comes to be seen how great are the possessions believers have in common.

The *Constitution on the Church* describes hopes that can be realized only if the *Constitution on the Sacred Liturgy* comes fully into force. Conversely, the liturgy document has the possibility of being effective in Catholic circles only on the supposition that there will be immediate implementation of the *Constitution on the Church* and the decree *On Ecumenism.*

29. It's the Law!

We who bear the name "Christian" are never free to forget the struggle Jesus had with men who said that religion was largely a matter of keeping laws.

He himself was unalterably committed to keeping God's Law, mind you. He was not out to abolish it but to fulfill its smallest letter, even its smallest part of a letter. (Listen to Matthew 5, 17–18, the next time it is read out at Mass on the feast of a Doctor of the Church.)

For Jesus, the Law given through Moses was His heavenly Father's teaching. His words are that no least part of it is to be "done away with until it all comes true." Jesus spent His whole public career teaching the Law, upholding it, making it come true.

The laws of men were a different thing entirely. Our Lord's criticisms were directed against a set of interpretations worked out by rabbis over the previous several centuries—a "hedge around the Law," in their own phrase—the minute observance of which (they said) rendered a man just in God's eyes.

Our Lord maintained that nothing of the sort was true. The weightier precepts of the Law for Him were justice and mercy and good faith, not taxes levied on garden herbs or rules for washing cups and bowls. (Read Matthew 23, 23–25.)

His struggle, therefore, was not against a teaching delivered by His Father on Mount Sinai. How could it be? It was against an outlook that clung fast to the Law, developed it in endless detail, and held the keeping of it to be the way of salvation, yet which all the while went against the spirit and intent of the Law. The Law had the meaning God invested it with, the Savior insisted. That meaning was one of love and service. Jesus, far from destroying the Law, sent the Spirit from His Father's side to help men keep it in its fullness.

The thread of rigidity, formalism, and legislation for the

sake of law-making is by no means a Jewish phenomenon. Such attitudes have always plagued the Church as well. To set the Law (Mosaic religion) in opposition to the Gospel (Christian religion) without further qualification is to misread the two testaments of Scripture thoroughly. There were, you will find, numerous persons who trusted in God's gracious power to save them under the Law—the prophets, for example, and later the pious poor—while the Christian community was far from free of those who thought they could be saved by the performance of certain specified good works laid down in laws.

So great is the Church's struggle to be free of *legalism* (not law, which can be a good thing if one counts on the Holy Spirit's aid in keeping it), that one hesitates long before he says: "Obey the *Constitution on the Sacred Liturgy*. It's the law!" That kind of argument strikes one as unworthy of the one whom we call Master. Yet this document of Vatican II which regulates the Church's prayer life contains the loving instruction given by teachers in the Church, about whom Jesus said—in the person of His original twelve—"He who hears you hears me."

"It's the law" means, in this case, a spelling out of the terms on which the whole Western Church is to pray. "Under Christ her head" is, of course, understood, but in this teaching we are given specific forms of prayer and told that faithfulness to them is especially calculated to bring us into one under His headship.

There is a canon in the Code of Canon Law, number 1257, which says, "It pertains to the Apostolic See alone to order the sacred liturgy and to approve the liturgical books." This law (1918) summed up the development of many centuries on the question. Just as all the action of the Mass had gone by default to the celebrant (except the contributions of servers and choir), so all regulation of how the mysteries were to be celebrated had gone by default to the men gathered around the Bishop of Rome. The correction of abuses and superstitious practices in prayer, which Canon 1261 says the individual bishop must see to, comprises the sole exception to this.

Even though the whole body of bishops—the apostolic college assembled in union with the chief bishop—possesses supreme power over the universal Church (Canon 228:1) in matters of worship as in other matters, in practice the chief bishop alone had the say up until December 4, 1963. On that day the world's bishops put Canon 228:1 into force in this one area at least.

That is why the chief thing the *Constitution* did about worship, we may say, is take the overseeing of it from the pope's hands, and put it into those of the bishops—with the pope's approval needless to say. The reasons given for this action are the ancient ones about the spiritual power bishops have. The Church, for example, is defined as "the holy people united and ordered under their bishops" (Article 26), and the individual bishop of a diocese "is to be considered as the high priest of his flock, from whom the life in Christ of his faithful is in some way derived and dependent." (Article 41)

These being the realities in the case, it is a puzzle how the high priest came to have nothing to say about the conduct of his people at prayer. Before the *Constitution* he was even less well-situated than an abbot or a provincial of religious clergy in dispensing his priests from praying the divine office in special circumstances!

Well, all this is changed now. The new, balanced situation is described in Article 22,1: "Regulation of the sacred liturgy depends solely on the authority of the Church, that is, on the Apostolic See and, as laws may determine, on the bishop." That phrase, "Apostolic See," means that the regulation of worship forms is still a papal concern just as heretofore. What is new is the word "bishop" in the singular, meaning that each bishop has an authority and power to regulate which had not been his to exercise for many centuries. That all the bishops together had such power no one doubted (see Canon 228:1), but that they should have wished to exercise it singly or in large regional groups once more is a restoration of ancient practice.

When Pope Pius XII wrote about this question in *Mediator Dei* (1947) he restricted discretionary power to "the supreme pontiff alone." Pope Paul VI in his apostolic letter *Sacram Liturgiam* (January 25, 1964), which named the date the *Con-*

stitution should go into effect (February 16, 1964), said that whenever legitimately established territorial bodies of bishops were spoken of—as in Article 22,2 of the *Constitution*—the term should be taken, for now, to be understood as meaning national hierarchies.

Now, where does all this leave us? First of all, the bishops of the world left the spelling-out of the implications of the *Constitution,* which they wrote, to a commission of forty members headed by Cardinal Giacomo Lercaro of Bologna. When this body gets out an instruction, as it did on September 26, 1964, naming March 7, 1965, as the date by which all dioceses were to conform, the bishops of the West are on record that they mean to conform. It is, after all their commission to help execute their law. The Holy See has a part in this through Pope Paul's having asked his Sacred Congregation of Rites to co-sponsor the document, as it were.

At times the instruction will say that a certain matter is left up to the individual bishop to decide (for example, whether the celebrant shall preside over the liturgy of the word from the pulpit or lectern or the presidential chair). But it is not left up to individual bishops to decide whether the celebrants shall be at one of these three places rather than at the altar. This matter the document settles. It is the law.

There may be an individual pastor who is unhappy with "all these new changes" but he is no more expected to disregard them than his bishop is. Thus, when a bishop decides that, in his diocese, his people can receive the holy eucharist under two species on such and such occasions (which he specifies out of the ten possibilities given in the law), or that his priests shall concelebrate at the annual retreat or during a diocesan synod, no pastor is expected to say, "You'll never catch me doing that."

The expectation throughout the Church is that bishops will remain faithful to their own law as passed by their overwhelming vote, and to the Holy See; that pastors will remain faithful to the law of their own bishop or the law of all the bishops of their country; and that people will be faithful to the law that their pastors pass along to them. It is needless to say that no bishop or priest or parishioner needs anyone's permission to

keep the general law of the Church. It's like being a citizen of
the United States or of Montana or of Cook County. You're
rather expected to!

Jesus left His friends and followers a heritage of love and
obedience, not a heritage of law. But even the obedient need
guidance. Those who don't obey, or don't obey readily (alas!),
need directions for their own good and everyone else's. Result: laws *in* the Church, laws *of* the Church. The *Constitution* is such a law; so is the U.S. bishops' decree of April 2,
1964, about language in the liturgy; so is the conciliar instruction of September 26, 1964; so is a bishop's directive about
how the sacraments will be celebrated in his diocese.

People like to say about civil rights (or obscene literature or
union activity), "You can't legislate morality." That's quite
true if it means you can't change human hearts by threats of
fine or imprisonment. You can legislate to keep Negroes from
being beaten up by police, though, or to stop the dope traffic.

In the same way, Church law of itself will never bring about
love for celebrating the mystery of Christ by way of full participation. If there is no understanding of the law, it can even
threaten such love. But when you have a whole Catholic population that is ready to love and serve, then laws about liturgy
are helpful. Jesus himself did not hesitate to say, "If you love
me, keep my commands."

30. There Has to Be Renewal
if It Really Is Christ's Church

All during the past year the columns of the country's newspapers, daily and religious, have been popping with reports about renewal and change in the Church. At the same time, the most obvious thing about the Catholic press is that it is published by people who are true to the ancient faith. They are Catholic to the core—yet they don't want things to continue in the Church precisely as they have been in the immediate past. In this, they stand shoulder to shoulder with the bishops of the Church who in Council are doing something about it, no matter what their individual approaches may be.

The test of loyalty to Christ and His Church is twofold: One hopes, with the help of God's grace, never to depart from Christ's person or His teaching until death, and one never rests satisfied with the state of His Church in any period of history.

This essential Catholic loyalty is important on two counts. If you think Christ is anything less than the fullness of God's communication with men, or if you are afraid He may leave His Church in the lurch one day, then you don't believe in the *Christ* of Catholic faith. If, at the same time, you are not convinced the Church is made up of sinful men who need to be repenting, changing, and improving constantly, then you don't believe in the *Church* of Catholic faith.

There is a narrow, partisan outlook which goes on the theory, "If it's Catholic, it's right." Now if that were only to mean, "If it's according to the mind of Christ—impelled by the Spirit of Jesus—it's right," you couldn't say there was anything narrow or partisan about it.

That would describe much that happens in the human family both within and without the confines of the Catholic Church. Usually, though, this mentality means to say, "If

Catholic people did it, it's right," or "If it happened in the Church in my youth, it's especially right."

Here is a serviceable yardstick or norm to help determine what is changeable and unchangeable in the Church. In the measure that a belief or practice is of Christ, it cannot be changed. In the measure that it is of men, it should be changed regularly. This is both because man's needs change, and because being a sinner man is capable of abuses in conducting the affairs of the Church.

The progress made in science, communication, political structures, and the like places new requirements on Christians in every age. At the same time, schism, heresy, nationalism, and war bring about painful separation among men and demand their continued efforts toward unity and peace.

For all these reasons, the task of reforming human institutions in the Church is never-ending. There are ever so many of these institutions because the Church is composed of men. In fact, aside from the Christian mysteries themselves, there are no other institutions in the Church! Any time the Church supposes she is in exactly the same condition of blessedness as her head, Christ, she will begin to fail in the necessary business of calling on Him to reform her.

The one comforting thing about believing in Christ's Church is that you never feel you're in this thing alone. The Spirit is ever available to the Church if only it will call on Him. If Christ says—as He does in the book with which the Bible closes—"I make all things new" (Apoc. 21,5), He means to achieve this newness through the agency of the Spirit whom He has sent from the Father. Renewal is a lively possibility only if what exists in the first place is that ever-to-be-renewed organism which is the dwelling place of God among men, the Church of His love.

Many times in the last four or five years Protestant Christians have observed that the Council is achieving an interior reform which they have found hard to accomplish in their own bodies. This is the world turned upside down, for the Protestant groups came into existence because their leaders despaired that the Roman Church ever could or would reform herself. By the time Trent was convened (1545), the gulf between Catholics and Reformers was already too wide to be closed over readily; the latter were not invited to partake as full members in the Council, as they wished. It was a Council of Catholics *against* Reformers—even though it enacted many things into law that the Reformers had been struggling for. Then there was the sad fact that many of the reforms that became Church law at Trent weren't enforced because the Church didn't have enough bishops who either could understand or wished to understand all the changes.

In debates of commissions before the First Council of the Vatican (1869–1870) elaborate preparations were made for reforms that were never enacted. Small pieces of important work were done in the plenary sessions on the office of the pope and on the fact of revelation. Because of all that wasn't done, this fragmentary achievement proved harmful to Christian unity almost in equal measure as helpful over the next ninety years.

For these reasons, the Church of Christ which is our mother —always open to the possibility of inner reform—didn't get much reform through the normal channels for a period of four hundred years. By normal channels we mean frequent ecumenical councils or even large regional synods (another word for meetings).

Some wonderful providential care was shown to the Church in the person of the Roman bishops from Leo XIII to John XXIII. But no one expects or should expect a single bishop—even though he is the man in Peter's see—to be as wise alone as all the Catholic bishops of Christendom together. There just isn't anything in human affairs to be compared to an open-floor debate and it is on this principle that the Church has operated since New Testament times.

When men of great convictions share their experience of the reality of God's action in their lives with others, great good is bound to come of it. You can't beat the technique. In fact, ever since the Council of Jerusalem (Acts 15, Gal. 2), the occasion of some serious differences among the Apostles which were resolved in charity, the Church hasn't had any technique but that of the face-to-face confrontation of bishops.

The surprise which Protestants have registered has been owing to their conviction that we Catholics have forgotten a corrective device built into the very make-up of the Church. We hadn't forgotten it, of course; we had just grown very rusty in its use. The one important difference between Church meetings generally and ecumenical councils of the churches in communion with the Church at Rome is that the bishops who gather there bind themselves by the decrees they draw up.

They are convinced that their joint conclusions really are a "voice of God." Therefore, even the bishops who vote against certain matters go home knowing that the outcome is either the faith of the Church or else her binding discipline. They mean to live by all they enact, if they understand it and if their own lives aren't seriously in need of reform.

That last possibility was the sadness that marked the period immediately after Trent. You can't have a reform if you haven't got bishops who know what reforms are needed, and are anxious to get on with them. St. Charles Borromeo, the Archbishop of Milan, was one who knew what needed doing and got busy at it with a right good will. His type wasn't too numerous, however. The great reformers before and after Trent tended to be the lower clergy (like the Jesuits and others). And the way the Church is arranged by the will of Christ, no one—repeat, no one—but a bishop can really get this job done.

The Church is blessed with some great, reformer bishops in our day. You can see that by reading *Council Speeches of Vatican II* (ed. Congar, Küng, O'Hanlon, Paulist, 1964). Will they prevail? One hopes so. The Holy Spirit will never desert His Church. That much is sure. The only faithfulness in question is that of all of us in the Church—bishops, priests, and people—to Christ.

Will they be faithful to Him? Will we be faithful to Him?

If so, then the Church is, in a sense, already reformed in seed and root and branch.

Scriptural Citations

Index

ECHO BOOKS

ECHO BOOKS are a series of popularly written paperbound books of Catholic interest for the modern reader. All areas of literature are to be represented in the series—fiction, non-fiction, biography, autobiography, Church history, the Bible, lives of great Catholics, Church doctrine, and works of a spiritual nature. The aim of ECHO BOOKS is to offer worthwhile books of Catholic appeal that will provide wholesome, informative, entertaining, and inspirational reading in inexpensive paperbound editions.

ECHO BOOKS was chosen as the name of the series as it is our hope that these books will echo, through popular literature, the word of God and the teachings of the Catholic Church.

We welcome the comments and suggestions of ECHO BOOKS readers at all times. A circular describing all the ECHO BOOKS available may be obtained from your nearest bookseller or directly from the publisher.　　　E 1

Other
ECHO BOOKS
for every reading taste . . .

DATING FOR YOUNG CATHOLICS
by Msgr. George A. Kelly
A straightforward guide for Catholic teen-agers on the "do's" and "don'ts" of dating and other social activities.
E11—75¢

THE SHROUD
by John Walsh
with 12 pages of illustrations
The amazing story of the cloth which many believe is the burial shroud of Jesus Christ.
E12—85¢

A CHILD OF MIRACLES
*by Frederic P. Gehring, C.M.
with Martin Abramson*
The incredible story of six-year-old Patsy Li, lost in a ship's bombing off Singapore, as told by the Padre of Guadalcanal.
E13—85¢

PLEASANT COMPANY ACCEPTED
by Rita Anton
with 18 linecuts
A charming and nostalgic collection of essays on family life written with wit, charm, and affection.
E14—75¢

SAINT CATHERINE LABOURÉ OF THE MIRACULOUS MEDAL
by Joseph I. Dirvin, C.M.
The definitive biography of St. Catherine Labouré and the story of Our Lady's appearances to her with the Miraculous Medal.
E15—85¢

ANGEL OF THE DELTA
by Edward F. Murphy
An inspiring biographical novel of a woman famed for her goodness and charity in nineteenth-century New Orleans.
E16—85¢

FATHER FLANAGAN OF BOYS TOWN
by Fulton Oursler and Will Oursler
The warm human story of a man's devotion to an ideal and his unshakable faith in human nature.
E17—95¢

SISTER CLARE
by Loretta Burrough
A novel telling of the joys, hardships, struggles, and fulfillment of a cloistered nun in the Carmelite order.
E18—85¢

AMEDEO
by Daphne Barclay
The poignant story of a twelve-year-old boy's search for the mother he never knew. "A lovely story of simple, sensible, deeply-Catholic principled people."—*America*
E19—75¢

THE BUMP ON BRANNIGAN'S HEAD
by Myles Connolly
An amusing yarn, by the author of Mr. Blue, about the overwhelming effects of Christian love.
E20—75¢

If your bookseller is unable to supply certain titles, write to Echo Books, Department MEB, Garden City, New York, stating the titles you desire and enclosing the price of each book (plus 5¢ per book to cover cost of postage and handling). Prices are subject to change without notice.

E 3

32H

ECHO BOOKS

Popularly written, informative, entertaining,
and inspirational books of Catholic
interest for the modern reader

THE ROAD LESS TRAVELED

by Richard Belair

A novel of a young man's journey to the priesthood and his experiences in the seminary.

E21—75¢

BLACK ROBE: The Life of Pierre-Jean DeSmet—missionary, explorer, and pioneer

by John Upton Terrell

A biography of the Jesuit priest who explored the uncharted West during the mid-19th century.

E22—85¢

THE LIVELY ARTS OF SISTER GERVAISE

by John L. Bonn, S.J.

A sprightly novel about a nun teaching high school who becomes involved in everything from dramatics and dances to teen-age crushes and family woes.

E23—75¢

MY BROTHERS, REMEMBER MONICA

by Patricia McGerr

A deeply moving novel about the mother of St. Augustine and how her indomitable faith gave the Church one of its greatest saints.

E24—85¢

DEDE O'SHEA

by Peggy Goodin

The delightful adventures and misadventures of an irresistible eleven-year-old who will steal anyone's heart away.

E25—75¢

SALT OF THE EARTH: An Informal Portrait of Richard Cardinal Cushing

by John H. Fenton

A lively, informative biography of Boston's popular, unpredictable Cardinal Cushing from his birth to his present international fame.

E26—95¢

THERESE: Saint of a Little Way

*New and Revised Edition
by Frances Parkinson Keyes*

A popular biography about the Little Flower in which St. Therese emerges as a living symbol for today's Christian.

E27—75¢

FLAME OUT OF DORSET

by Clifford Stevens

A novel about a 20th-century Trappist priest, St. Stephen Harding—founder of the Trappist Order, and a mysterious meeting with a 700-year-old monk.

E28—75¢

If your bookseller is unable to supply certain titles, write to Echo Books, Department MEB, Garden City, New York, stating the titles you desire and enclosing the price of each book (plus 5¢ per book to cover cost of postage and handling). Prices are subject to change without notice.

Other

ECHO BOOKS

for every reading taste . . .

TWO TO GET READY
by Henry V. Sattler, C.SS.R.
A practical book on marriage and its preparation aimed at the "younger set". **E29—75¢**

NO TWO ALIKE
Those Maryknoll Sisters!
by Sister Maria del Rey
True stories about Maryknoll sisters and their experiences and daily activities in missionary life. **E30—85¢**

CATHOLICS COURAGEOUS
Foreword by Richard Cardinal Cushing
by Alfred K. Allan
Twenty-seven actual stories of contemporary Catholics whose faith enabled them to overcome personal difficulties and give inspiration to others. **E31—75¢**

WORSHIP IN A NEW KEY
by Gerard S. Sloyan
A comprehensive explanation of the Council's Constitution on the Sacred Liturgy written for the average layman. **E32—75¢**

THE MAN WHO CAPTIVATED NEW YORK
by Rosalie Lieberman
A novel about the adventures of Brother Angelo who brings faith and happiness to lonely people. **E33—75¢**

YESTERDAY, TODAY, AND FOREVER
by Maria Augusta Trapp
The author of The Story of the Trapp Family Singers explains how she and her husband took the Holy Family as their model for their own family life.
E34—85¢

FATHER HILARY'S HOLIDAY
by Bruce Marshall
A novel about the escapades of Father Hilary Hopkins who turns an "ecumenical" visit to a mythical country into a whacky holiday. **E35—75¢**

THE TIBER WAS SILVER
by Michael Novak
The story of the inner-struggle of Richard McKay, a 25-year-old American seminarian student in Rome, to decide between the priesthood and a career as a painter. **E36—85¢**

If your bookseller is unable to supply certain titles, write to Echo Books, Department MEB, Garden City, New York, stating the titles you desire and enclosing the price of each book (plus 5¢ per book to cover cost of postage and handling). Prices are subject to change without notice.